"*American Restoration* is a clarion call to truly making America great again, by making America good again. It is a timely, prescient reminder that the Judeo-Christian morals upon which the nation was based remain the most solid foundation for our shining city on the hill—and that only a re-engagement with those moral foundations will allow us to build to new heights."

—**BEN SHAPIRO**, editor in chief, the Daily Wire

"There's no question that the heart and soul of America are ailing. It's easy to become discouraged and to believe that our country's best days are behind it. In *American Restoration*, however, Tim Goeglein and Craig Osten paint a hopeful picture of the future that lies ahead if the people of this great nation will do the hard work necessary to restore freedom, family, and self-sacrifice to the center of America's values."

—**JIM DALY**, president, Focus on the Family

"Over two centuries ago, pundits both within and outside the United States praised the new nation as a shining beacon of hope for its own people and for the rest of the world. Yet today, public opinion polls, media commentary, and everyday conversations reveal the concern that our nation is losing its finest qualities and faces a bleak future. In *American Restoration*, Tim Goeglein and Craig Osten present a brilliant analysis of our current fight and provide a commonsense blueprint to recover and perpetuate the principles, ideals, and spiritual values that are the foundation of a beneficial culture. This highly readable book will inspire and enlighten a dedicated citizenry to seek and fulfill the promise that our Founders envisioned."

—**EDWIN MEESE III**, 75th United States Attorney General

"When I speak about my book *If You Can Keep It: The Forgotten Promise of American Liberty*, people inevitably ask 'What can I do?' And 'How can I help turn the cultural tide and "keep the republic"?' Now I have a simple response. Read this excellent book, which has many of the answers to those vitally important questions."

—**ERIC METAXAS**, *New York Times* #1 bestselling author of *Bonhoeffer* and *Martin Luther*

"As Christians, we are called to convey hope. And that is what my friends Tim Goeglein and Craig Osten do in *American Restoration*. They provide a blueprint that not only provides hope, but will help return America to the principles upon which it was founded, that all men have an unalienable right from their Creator to life, liberty, and the pursuit of happiness. The restoration of these God-given principles, as outlined in this book, will once again make America a shining city on a hill for the world to see."

—**ALAN SEARS**, founder, Alliance Defending Freedom

"In *American Restoration*, Tim and Craig expertly outline some of the most pressing issues of this century and provide a roadmap based on our founding principles to repair the very fabric of this nation."

—**KAY COLES JAMES**, president, the Heritage Foundation

"This book is like a blueprint for those who love their neighbors and wish to see a nation in which that which is true, good, and beautiful is able to flourish. It's full of wisdom from the past and hope for the future."

—**JOHN STONESTREET**, president, the Chuck Colson Center for Christian Worldview

AMERICAN RESTORATION

AMERICAN RESTORATION

HOW FAITH, FAMILY, AND PERSONAL SACRIFICE CAN HEAL OUR NATION

TIMOTHY S. GOEGLEIN & CRAIG OSTEN

REGNERY GATEWAY

Regnery Gateway™ is a registered trademark of Salem Communications Holding Corporation

Regnery® is a registered trademark of Salem Communications Holding Corporation

Cataloging-in-Publication data on file with the Library of Congress

ISBN 978-1-62157-911-3
ebook ISBN 978-1-62157-912-0

Published in the United States by ·
Regnery Gateway, an imprint of
Regnery Publishing
A Division of Salem Media Group
300 New Jersey Ave NW
Washington, DC 20001
www.RegneryGateway.com

Manufactured in the United States of America ·

10 9 8 7 6 5 4 3 2 1

Books are available in quantity for promotional or premium use. For information on discounts and terms, please visit our website: www.Regnery.com.

Note: The opinions offered in this book are those of the authors and do not necessarily represent the views and positions of their employers.

From Tim Goeglein:

For Jenny, Tim, Paul, Beverly, and Stanley: You are the loves of my life and you continue to show me that the best life is the one enveloped in unconditional love, given and received. Soli Deo Gloria!

From Craig Osten:

For my wife, daughter, son-in-law, and three precious grandchildren. May you continue to enjoy the God-given liberties that made our nation great and allowed true freedom to flourish.

Contents

"The…conservative is concerned, first of all, for the regeneration of spirit and character…with the perennial problem of the inner order of the soul, the restoration of the ethical understanding, and the religious sanction upon which any life worth living is founded. This is conservatism at its highest." [1]

—Russell Kirk

"Conservatism starts from the sentiment that all mature people can readily share: the sentiment that good things are easily destroyed, but not easily created. This is especially true of the good things that come to us as collective assets: peace, freedom, law, civility, public spirit, the security of property, and family life, in all of which we depend on the cooperation of others while having no means singlehandedly to obtain it. In respect of such things, the work of destruction is quick, easy, and exhilarating; the work of creation slow, laborious, and dull." [2]

—Roger Scruton

"If we take the widest and wisest view of a Cause, there is no such thing as a Lost Cause, because there is no such thing as a Gained Cause. We fight for lost causes because we know that our defeat and dismay may be the preface to our successor's victory, though that victory itself will be temporary; we fight rather to keep something alive than in the expectation that it will triumph." [3]

—T. S. Eliot

"The World is trying the experiment of attempting to form a civilized but non-Christian mentality. The experiment will fail; but we must be very patient in awaiting its collapse; meanwhile redeeming the time: so that the Faith may be preserved alive through the dark ages before us; to renew and rebuild civilization, and save the World from suicide." [4]

—T. S. Eliot

"One of the first symptoms they discover of a selfish and mischievous ambition is a profligate disregard of a dignity which they partake with others. To be attached to the subdivision, to love the little platoon we belong to in society, is the first principle (the germ as it were) of public affections. It is the first link in the series by which we proceed towards a love to our country, and to mankind. The interest of that portion of social arrangement is a trust in the hands of all those who compose it; and as none but bad men would justify it in abuse, none but traitors would barter it away for their own personal advantage." [5]

—Edmund Burke

"At least five times…the Faith has to all appearances gone to the dogs. In each of these five cases, it is the dog that died." [6]

—G. K. Chesterton

"The task of redeeming Western society rests in a peculiar sense upon Christianity." [7]

—Reinhold Niebuhr

"The people who know their God shall stand firm and take action."
—Daniel 11:32b, English Standard Version (ESV)

Prologue

One of the most common and recurring conversations across America today is the fate of our country's culture. There is a belief in some quarters the United States has now passed its maturity and started the long, slow decline to eventual death. As a nation, we have divided ourselves into "red" and "blue" camps that bicker at each other like two elderly men playing checkers in the park.

The result is many Americans have concluded that, like many other great civilizations, our nation is crumbling from within. Many surmise that our physical, moral, and cultural infrastructure—once the envy of the world—is dying a slow death of abuse and neglect.

In their view, our institutions have become not only rigid, sclerotic, and unresponsive, but also openly hostile to the Judeo-Christian values that served as the basis of America's foundation. Our educational system seems to undermine deliberately the values parents are trying to instill in their children while cranking out graduates who can barely read or write, let alone critically think about any issue. Our national debt is out of control, leaving a legacy of crippling financial nightmares for our children and grandchildren. Generations of children have never known the loving stability of the two-parent home, resulting in a continually downward spiral of hopelessness, poverty, and despair.

Most of all, many perceive there is no cultural agreement on even the most fundamental issues of values and morality, which are left more to individual whim than national consensus. This has resulted in a national discourse often so vile and venomous it seems to be beyond repair.

To those who observe these breakdowns, America's demise seems imminent. Much like an aged and diseased body, our foundational institutions—along with our respect and civility toward each other—are withering. Thus, for approximately half the country, a sense of hopelessness and impending doom permeates the land because they perceive that we, as a nation, are abandoning faith-based values. For the other half, they believe the future will only be bright if we completely abandon what they perceive to be "oppressive" and "regressive" elements of American society—namely, our Judeo-Christian heritage—and put our faith in government solutions for every aspect of our lives. They have a feeling of doom and gloom because we are not abandoning that heritage or embracing an all-encompassing government fast enough.

This fatalism is lamentable. Those who argue that we have abandoned our Judeo-Christian heritage have come to accept that there is no reason to believe our nation is exempt from the larger historical forces of decadence. In their minds, America's historical moment in the sun has ended and darkness is rapidly approaching. They have concluded that the 250-year great American experiment in ordered liberty—while representing a glorious and unprecedented chapter in world history—is fundamentally over. In their minds, America's visionary and revolutionary form of government—the constitutional republic—is wheezing down the road like an old car. And rather than try to squeeze a few more miles out of it and risk a complete breakdown, it may be time to trade it in for a new model—whatever that model may be.

For those on the other side of the debate, that 250-year experiment cannot end quickly enough. They despair that people continue to cling to what they view as outdated belief systems and impede what they perceive to be progress in achieving their vision of a utopian society.

Is this truly America's fate? Has our nation reached the end of its life span, destined unavoidably to pass away in the near future? Or could it experience a restoration? What acts of renewal can we take in our personal and national lives to help bring about this regeneration?

These are the questions we seek to answer in this book. Unlike those who believe America is staring helplessly at the raised blade of the Grim Reaper for our nation, we take a more hopeful view. We believe American restoration is not only possible, but also probable, if we act now.

We do not subscribe to the "Benedict Option," at least as it is understood by many: the retreat of Christians into private communities to await the inevitable collapse of a corrupt society, eventually reemerging to rebuild it.[8] While we would agree that the foundations of our society are indeed in a state of decay, there is much we can still do to restore those foundations in our communities and reverse the decay before it is too late.

There has been a great deal of debate over the Benedict Option in political and academic circles. Its author, Rod Dreher, insists that he is not calling for a total Christian withdrawal from politics or the broader culture, but is calling on Christians to strengthen their families and faith communities so they can survive the dark times that are upon us.

The purpose of this book is not to debate Dreher's thesis, but to suggest that regardless of what he is advocating, this is not a time for good people of faith to withdraw completely from society.

While we would agree the signs of decadence that were part of the Roman Empire are now real and inarguable here in America, we also believe we can arrest that decay and commence an American restoration before it is too late. To do so requires us to understand this is not a time for withdrawal, but instead a time to engage, to continue to be "salt and light." Therefore, we must remain involved in our communities to transform hearts and lives while remaining engaged nationally to help slow and reverse the decay occurring in those same communities because of the negative impact of policy decisions at the state and federal levels. Thus, with regard to calling on Christians to be intentional about their faith, we have no quibble. Many of the issues we face today are because Christians have not been intentional with their faith in their interactions with others and their engagement with their communities.

Our engagement must come with the understanding that restoration and renewal have to come from within. In the words of the late Chuck Colson, "Salvation will not come on Air Force One." Even in days when we had national leaders—such as Franklin Roosevelt, Dwight Eisenhower, John F. Kennedy, and Ronald Reagan—who affirmed America's Judeo-Christian heritage even when some of their policies or moral behavior may have not, our cultural decay continued on the local and state levels. This occurred as those seeking to destroy our Judeo-Christian foundations continued their assault virtually unabated in our schools, universities, city councils, and state capitols.

That is why we advocate for—as you will see throughout this book—people of faith to be involved in the private communities where real spiritual and cultural transformation occurs, engaging with their neighbors and co-workers while also remaining engaged in the public square. It is not an either-or proposition; it is both. If all of our focus is on national politics while our communities decay around us, we have failed in our mission. At the same time, if our communities are strong, but our national politics make it harder and harder for us to practice our faith, to minister to others, and to have opportunities to succeed, then we have failed in our mission, as well.

The renewal for which we speak, hope, advocate, and pray for must be rooted in a reconciliation between the great Judeo-Christian ethos and secular culture. This reconciliation will involve the reweaving of our nation's tattered and fraying national tapestry into a new garment that once again includes the virtues of faith, family, and personal sacrifice that made America the beacon of hope it has been for the world—the nation the "teeming masses" from around the world traveled to for freedom and prosperity. We believe there are various specific acts of renewal that all of us can participate in to make this national restoration possible. Some are very simple; some will take greater effort. But collectively, they can bring transformation.

When we express this view, we sometimes receive vast skepticism. Powering that skepticism is a deeply felt conviction that our national decline will take a long time, dragging along for decades like a grand dowager trying harder and harder to stop the relentless ravages of advancing age.

In our understanding, the West evolved into a civilization with two sources of authority—one divine, the other secular. The first source is the norms and values of Christianity. The second, secular source is rational enlightenment. These two sources—while radically different—acknowledged there were key moral principles and norms upon which healthy societies are built. They also held a joint belief in the existence of a higher authority than our own and the belief that individuals should be free to worship as they choose. It was the acknowledgement of this authority that served as the glue of our civilization.

Unfortunately, many in today's elite political and cultural world are working overtime to deconstruct America's Judeo-Christian foundation. While America's history is not perfect—particularly in the area of slavery, and later civil rights—our culture, imperfect as it may be, still had faith in God and the moral principles laid out in Scripture as its foundation.

The authority that foundation was based on now finds itself replaced by a radical secularism and propulsive postmodernism that rejects with a frightful degree those moral principles. American culture has gone from commending the righteous to condemning them. Too often, vice is celebrated while virtue is disdained.

Thus, faith—previously seen as a positive element in society—is increasingly belittled and openly mocked. Extramarital sex and cohabitation are perceived as normal, and those who believe in faith-based standards for sexual behavior are seen as abnormal. Because of this paradigm shift, this new order possesses a particular animus against people who still adhere to the teachings and values of their faith, particularly conservative Evangelicals, Catholics, Mormons, and Jews.

By striking at those norms and values, this new order seeks to eradicate our Judeo-Christian heritage. Ultimately, it is striking at the very essence of liberty itself. Thus, in recent years at our nation's college and university campuses, those who call for tolerance and free speech are actively demonizing and censoring those with whose free speech and beliefs they disagree, thereby showing a lack of tolerance. Groups finding themselves outside the current campus orthodoxy—such as Christian ministries, conservative limited government groups, and others—are denied the ability to even exist.

As James Kurth, professor emeritus of political science at Swarthmore College, put it, "The real clash will not be between the West and one or more of the Rest. It will be between the West and the Post-West, within the West itself."[9] Or, as it has been put many times by others and documented in history, all great civilizations die not because of an attack by an outside enemy, but because of decay within.

Alexis de Tocqueville understood this as well, writing, "Religion in America takes no direct part in the government of society, but it must be regarded as the first of their political institutions; for if it does not impart a taste for freedom, it facilitates the use of [freedom]." [10] Thus, in his view, without faith at the foundation of a nation, freedom cannot flourish.

In our human understanding, the landscape does look bleak and the horizon even more so. We inhabit a culture largely shaped by elites who often see themselves as intellectually superior to the "masses" and who reject objective truth while propelling and embracing normlessness and meaninglessness. Nevertheless, we believe there is hope and a better way forward for the United States.

David Brooks, writing in the *New York Times*, provides a succinct summary of the differences between those who believe America's best days are behind us and those who think our nation's best days are yet to come. He calls the two camps "upswingers" and "downswingers." He writes that upswingers believe in progress while downswingers have lost faith in progress. As a result, they feel everything is broken, and thus we must start all over again from scratch.

Brooks says upswingers and downswingers can be found on the Left and the Right. Regardless of political beliefs, downswingers are pessimists, and thus lash out in anger, despair, or hopeless resignation to their fate. Some have a great deal of distrust and are prone to conspiracy theories, while others may also lack civility and seek to silence any speech with which they do not agree.

He continues that while upswingers need to respect the critique of the downswingers, they cannot fall prey to pessimism. He argues there has to be economic, social, and political solidarity with those left behind, as well as "penance," in his words, for those who "did the leaving."

Finally, Brooks concludes that there must be a convincing story of where we are in history and a new moral order to affirm the dignity of those "who feel insulted." He says upswingers will have to conserve our basic institutions so they continue to produce real benefits while reforming them with "a hesitant radicalism," or moderation. He writes, "There are moments when society goes into decline. But there are many, many transitional moments when some just think society is in decline, when it is really a bumpy pivot. This is such a moment. It gets better."[11]

We concur with Brooks on this evaluation, even when we disagree with him on some substantive issues. If America returns to its spiritual foundations, we believe the tumultuous times we live in may be nothing more than a "bumpy pivot" in our nation's history.

We also concur with the late Neil Postman, who believed that after we exhaust ourselves with entertainment or amuse ourselves to death, as he so powerfully predicted, there would be a series of mini-rebellions among people who want other and better alternatives. We are beginning to see this ever so slightly with the elements of Generation Z and millennials and their quest for authenticity. While many have rejected the institutional church, they are seeking some sort of faith experience, but are still trying to figure out what that experience is.[12] It is our role to come alongside them, listen to them, and gently guide them to the authentic faith they seek.

For example, a recent phenomenon has been elements of these generations ditching their smart phones for old-school, no-frills "flip phones" that just provide the essential functions of calling and texting, and nothing else. After years of having the latest technology and information at their fingertips, young adults are finding out there are things far more important in life, such as making flesh and blood connections that encourage interaction with others, rather than digital ones, which do not.

We believe we have arrived at a pivotal moment in American history—a historic turning point where America will choose one direction or the other. Some feel we have already passed that point and there is no return. We have hope, but we thoroughly understand the scale of the battle. As Winston Churchill said so eloquently during the dark days after Dunkirk at the beginning of World War II—and Franklin Roosevelt reiterated later—we are fighting for the "survival of Christian civilization." [13] That is a civilization that sees every person as "*imago Dei*," made in the image of God.

We are in a battle for our civilization. And for many, the battlefield is filled with fire and despair, rather than hope. However, America also has associations of like-minded people and groups—such as churches and civic organizations, to name just two—who want a restored and healthier national culture and realize there is much we can do to bring about such a result.

The seeds of American regeneration are ready for sowing if we have the national will. These seeds, which in many ways can be thought of as a new counterculture, are alive in the arts, the military, the churches, the universities, and in the law.

They are even alive in politics. But most of all, these seeds can be found in the homes and communities of faithful Americans who still embrace the Judeo-Christian ethos upon which our nation was founded and seek to love their neighbors as Christ commands us.

Their faith is a confident, muscular Christianity that fuses faith and action, permeating every aspect of their lives, though it is often unseen or ignored. It is not a cruel faith, as it is often portrayed in the media. Instead, this faith is firm, rooted in ancient and unchanging reality, and strong enough to withstand the buffeting of changing social winds rooted in a timeless, unchanging, and transcendent moral order.

Our contemporary culture does not understand this kind of faith—indeed, no human culture has ever been able to grasp it. But the reality is it is this type of faith that will bring about the restoration of the society we seek, which T. S. Eliot described as one "in which the natural end of man-virtue and well-being in the community...is acknowledged by all, and the supernatural end—beatitude—for those who have the eyes to see it." [14]

We see glimpses of this society in our nation today, such as when a Christian furniture shop owner in Houston opens his showrooms so displaced people from Hurricane Harvey can sleep in the brand new beds he was planning to sell. [15] We see it when an infertile Christian couple decides to turn their personal heartbreak into ministry, opening their home to and raising six orphans of various races—children who simply want nothing more than a mom and a dad to call their own—and loving them unconditionally through all the peaks and valleys of their formative years. [16]

In July and August 2018, horrible wildfires swept through North Central California, resulting in numerous deaths and massive losses of property and destruction of land. Those affected by the wildfires felt hopeless as they saw everything they worked for go up in flames. The fire was started not by arsonists or careless campers, as is often the case, but by a blown tire on a trailer driven by an elderly couple. The flat tire caused sparks to fly as the exposed rim scraped the road, and one of the sparks ignited brush by the side of the road.

While the names of the elderly couple were not released, a woman named Rachel Pilli learned them from a firefighter at her church who said the couple were neighbors of his mother. They were grief-stricken about the damage caused because of the inadvertent accident, with the wife, in particular, feeling guilty because she asked her husband to take the trailer trip. According to the firefighter, the woman had been crying day and night on her sofa.

After hearing the story, Rachel, who works for a pro-life pregnancy center, decided to do something to help the elderly couple deal with their grief. She gave the firefighter a card expressing sympathy to the couple for the pain they were feeling.

But she did not stop there. Rachel also decided to reach out to her Facebook friends and ask them to send well-wishes she could forward to the couple. The next day, she read dozens of responses wishing the couple well—bringing tears to her eyes. Rachel said it was "an ocean of compassion, of love, and grace."

It continued. More and more people sent cards. A giant basket was received with envelopes and little gifts. A florist sent a bouquet. Rachel concluded, "I would think, no matter what race, what color, people are kind. Deep down I think that compassion and community are at the core of human beings. I think the fire has caused us to look in each other's eyes and discover the human kindness in us. . . . It's a beautiful story of hope and community." [17]

Such stories of service, compassion, and love arise from a distinct, recoverable religious foundation. This foundation is built upon what Edmund Burke called the "little platoons"—vibrant churches, fraternal groups, various neighborhood and community associations, and most importantly, strong, intact marriages and loving families.

These "little platoons" can play a critical role in restoring a robust civil society rooted in the common good where people understand that what happens in our homes, neighborhoods, and communities—coupled with a politically engaged and knowledgeable populace—will result in a thriving and healthy society.

Dependence on "little platoons" is a sharp contrast to the contemporary push to elevate the desires and demands of the individual over the well-being of the family, the community, and society as a whole. It was "little platoons" that led to groundswells that transformed society, whether it be the emerging Civil Rights Movement of the 1950s or the abolitionists who laid the pathway to abolish the sin of slavery. Neither one of these movements sprung from government, but from people of faith in their local communities.

Government will not ultimately provide the solutions we are so hungry for and, in some places, are so desperately needed. Instead, the solutions are already there in our churches, our communities, and above all, in our homes. It is our job to identify and begin to implement those solutions as "little platoons," which is what we seek to do in the following chapters.

So, let us all seek to be part of a "little platoon" in communities, working together to make a difference in our spheres of influence. The light illuminating our path and empowering us to succeed is our faith. As that light permeates the darkness, America will experience a reawakening, regeneration, and renewal that will restore true human flourishing from the tip of Maine to the rugged frontier of Alaska and everywhere in between.

CHAPTER ONE

Restoring America's Founding Principles

"In proportion as a society relaxes its hold upon the eternal, it ensures the corruption of the temporal. All earthly civilizations are indeed corruptible and must one day perish, the pax Britannica no less than the pax romana, and Christendom no less than Babylon or Troy. But if most have perished prematurely, it was largely as victims of their own proud illusions. And if our Western civilization is to prove more durable, it can only be in the strength of this most chastened estimate of its own majesty and this knowledge that 'here we have no continuing city.'" [1]

—John Baillie

"If a culture is to survive and flourish, it must not be severed from the religious vision out of which it arose." [2]

—Russell Kirk

"Should not the Bible regain the place it once held as a schoolbook? Its morals are pure, its examples are captivating and noble.... In no Book is there so good English, so pure and so elegant, and by teaching all the same they will speak alike, and the Bible will justly remain the standard of language as well as of faith." [3]

—Fisher Ames, contributor to the First Amendment

W e the authors (Tim and Craig) grew up in Indiana and California, respectively, during the 1960s and 1970s and during the cultural earthquake now known as the Sexual Revolution. Our experiences in these different states exposed us to two very different Americas.

1

Tim, growing up in Indiana in America's heartland, was more culturally removed from the tumult rocking other parts of the nation. In school and in church, he learned about America as a country founded by dissenting Protestants fleeing spiritual persecution in Europe. He learned that the Pilgrims of the Massachusetts Bay Colony saw their immigration to the New World as a retelling of the Exodus story—a reflection of the ancient Israelites' exodus from Egypt to freedom in the Promised Land. England, in this mode of thinking, was essentially an oppressive Egypt and the British monarchy was as Pharaoh was to the Jews.

Tim loved the vantage point he learned as a child. As he studied it further over the years, he discovered it to be true. The Atlantic Ocean was, to the Pilgrim fathers and mothers, as the Red Sea was to the escaping Israelites. Above all, America was the new Israel and the Native Americans were similar to the Canaanites. The Pilgrims eagerly and willingly left Europe to find spiritual liberty and build a new nation on principles rooted in the Bible.

Those who came to this new nation seeking religious freedom were not perfect, just as the escaping Israelites were not. They made some unfortunate and tragic mistakes in their treatment of the Native Americans. But they built this nation, as Tim's teachers taught, with the moral architecture of a Christian worldview consistent with the Judaic covenant with God, as well as the Ten Commandments God gave Moses on Mount Sinai. Had America not been constructed on this spiritual foundation, the outcome would have been very different.

However, Craig's experience was just the opposite. He grew up fifty miles north of San Francisco in the wine country of Sonoma County, where he witnessed the cutting edge of the deconstruction of biblical values. By the time he was seven, he was well aware of the cultural tumult going on. Every night via the evening news, he sat in his living room and watched the breakdown of law and order as the campus riots at UC Berkeley and San Francisco State University unfolded. While Craig learned the traditional Thanksgiving story in his early elementary school years, by the time he reached middle school in the early 1970s, the schools of Northern California taught a very different version of history.

Tim was not exposed to that version, which denounced the stories about our nation's biblical foundation as ridiculous fabrication, until he entered college at Indiana University. This new version promoted the idea the Pilgrims were European oppressors who destroyed the Native American culture and said that some American descendants of European immigrants had an obligation to apologize for the fact that our forefathers came to the shores of America in the first place. Rather than fleeing religious persecution, the Pilgrims in this version were the persecutors. This reinterpretation of history focused on the Pilgrims' faults, and not their virtues.

In addition, the narrative now said even if America was founded on Judeo-Christian principles, those principles themselves were unacceptable because they were reclassified as cultural oppression, which America needed to repent of and reject. In studying contemporary world affairs, this narrative said that whenever evil reared its ugly head around the world, it was often America's fault. Craig's ninth grade world history teacher, who later became the principal of his high school, hung portraits of Vladimir Lenin and Mao Zedong in his classroom and described them as sometimes misguided, but ultimately benevolent leaders. Later, in college, he had professors who insisted America's Founding Fathers were deplorable despots responsible for crimes against humanity and the Cold War was all America's fault.

This interpretation of American history comes from revisionist historian Howard Zinn, author of *A People's History of the United States*, which has served as content and curriculum material in our nation's public schools for the past four decades. Zinn depicts

America's founders—as Craig's teachers did—as oppressors, thieves, and tyrants who engaged in atrocities for their personal gain.

Over the same four decades, the two of us continued as students of history. Both of us did exactly what our revisionist instructors told us to do. We read about the founding of our country to come to a better understanding of its roots. Of course, the hope of those revisionist instructors was that by engaging in further study, we would agree with them. Instead, we both concluded that Tim's primary, secondary, and church teachers and Craig's early elementary school teachers were closer to the truth, and that our later teachers embraced a deeply flawed narrative.

However, as the saying goes, "Repeat a lie enough times, and it becomes the truth." That is what has happened to the teaching of American history, and particularly about the Judeo-Christian worldview upon which our nation was founded.

While we will expound more on America's educational system in a subsequent chapter, this rejection of and subsequent hostility regarding the facts of America's founding cuts to the root of all the national dilemmas we face today. Yes, America's founders—like many of us—were flawed individuals, and slavery was evil, unjust, and tragic. On that issue, there should be no doubt, and the shameful history of slavery and accompanying racism that has plagued our nation should be taught so it never occurs again. However, despite their flaws, they possessed a worldview based on knowledge of and respect for the Bible—a worldview that governed their decisions as they formed this nation. This worldview was best expressed in the Declaration of Independence as "life, liberty, and the pursuit of happiness."

Conservative commentator Dennis Prager, an observant Jew, has written eloquently about how the abandonment of biblical values has resulted in the societal chaos so many see happening. He says, "I have believed all my life that the primary crisis in America and the West is the abandonment of Judeo-Christian values, or as one might say, the dismissal of the Bible." [4]

He continued:

> Virtually everyone on the left thinks America would be better off as a secular nation. And virtually all conservative intellectuals don't think it matters.... And, yet, from the time long before the United States became a country until well into the 1950s, the Bible was not only the most widely read book in America—it was the primary vehicle by which an entire generation passed on morality and wisdom to the next generation. [5]

Prager postulates that over the past sixty years, America has gone from a Bible-based society to biblically ignorant. But in his view, even worse than biblical ignorance is the growing societal contempt for biblical principles. He writes, "Just about anyone who quotes the Bible, let alone says it's the source of his or her values, is essentially regarded as a simpleton who is anti-science, anti-intellectual, and sexist." [6]

In addition, we have observed the increasing encroachments on religious liberty—and all liberties—over the past sixty years. It is not a coincidence it has occurred in tandem with diminished virtue in society. There can be no liberty without virtue, and faith is the source from which virtue springs.

In subsequent chapters, we will discuss further thoughts on how faith is essential to each of America's institutions. Prager's basic argument is one we utterly agree with: without a biblically based foundation, we become morally confused and ultimately foolish. As the Apostle Paul wrote in 1 Corinthians 3:19, "For the wisdom of the world is foolishness in God's sight."

As mentioned previously, the Pilgrims and others who came to America from England saw themselves in the same light as the Jews who escaped Egypt. Abiel Abbot, an early pastor of First Church in Haverhill, Massachusetts, said in 1799, "the people of the United States come nearer to a parallel with Ancient Israel, than any other nation upon the globe. Hence our American Israel is a term frequently used and our common consent allows it apt and proper."[7] More recently, biblical scholar Gabriel Sivan wrote, "No Christian community in history identified more with the People of the Book than did the early settlers of the Massachusetts Bay Colony, who believed their own lives to be a literal enactment of the Biblical drama of the Hebrew nation."[8]

These observations are categorically consistent with letters, diaries, and primary sources from the Pilgrims and early American settlers. The key is not how those early Americans viewed themselves relative to the Bible and the ancient Jews, but why and how they saw the practical application of those principles to the creation, maintenance, and vitality of our government and civil society. In the early nineteenth century, no less an observer than Alexis de Tocqueville wrote that the centrality of authentic faith among Americans "should be considered the first of their political institutions."[9]

Tocqueville surmised that the widely held and mostly uncontested view in early America was the moral boundaries set out in Holy Scripture that provided the guardrails defining what was good and evil in the United States—all rooted in and deriving from those first Pilgrims' worldview. Americans believed God was the Author of our constitutional republic and His Providence was critical to a thriving democracy. Finally, he observed Americans purposely dismissed the views of those who were hostile to the Christian faith or who, in his words, "deride religion as nothing but a source of oppression and promote public atheism as a guarantee of freedom."[10]

Tocqueville reported firsthand on how these values shaped our nation, writing:

> But there is no other country in the whole world in which the Christian religion retains a greater influence over the souls of men than in America; and there can be no greater proof of its utility, and of its conformity to human nature, than that its influence is most powerfully felt over the most enlightened and free nation of the earth.[11]

Tocqueville did not ignore the evil he saw in America. He openly acknowledged the existence and evil of slavery. He knew America was a nation made up of sinful and imperfect human beings.

As Mark David Hall, Herbert Hoover Distinguished Professor of Politics and Faculty Fellow in the William Penn Honors Program at George Fox University, has written, America's Founders—as Tocqueville did—knew they were a nation of imperfect men. He writes that if the Founders agreed on anything, it was that humans were sinful. He quoted James Madison from *The Federalist* No. 51, writing, "If men were angels, no government would be necessary. If angels were to govern men, neither external nor internal controls on government would be necessary."

Hall states the Founders firmly believed in God-ordained moral standards, that legislation should be in accordance with those standards, and that moral laws take precedence over human laws.

Thus, in his view, the Founders' understanding of liberty was profoundly influenced by Christian morality—even if they were not Christians. He writes, "the Founders were far more likely to see liberty as the freedom to do what is morally correct." He quotes James Wilson, a signer of the Declaration of Independence and an early Supreme

Court justice, who said, "Law without liberty is tyranny, but liberty without law is licentiousness."

Hall states Wilson made it clear in his law lectures that the "law" in the second half of the quotation referred to God's moral law. He adds, "The Founders were not moral relativists," and concludes that while these views were not distinctly Christian, if one is to understand the principles upon which America was founded, it is "critical to recognize that most Founders were profoundly influenced by orthodox Christian theology." [12]

Dennis Prager comes to the same conclusion by noting one of our two greatest presidents (in his view) was Abraham Lincoln, who rarely attended church. However, Lincoln read the Bible daily and said, "In regards to this great book, I have but to say, I believe the Bible is the best gift God has given to man." [13] Even those who may not have been weekly worshippers still had great respect for the teachings and principles found within the Bible's pages and governed our nation as such.

It is because of this devotion to biblical principles that the Ten Commandments remain the seedbed of America's laws under which we, in the twenty-first century, are still governed. It is why Moses, holding the tablets upon which those commandments were written, is depicted as one of the great lawgivers on the walls of the United States Supreme Court.

The colonists and figures from America's early history believed communities with deep taproots in faith were the essential foundations in the new country they were founding. The importance of faith-based communities remained central to our nation's self-understanding until about the early-to-mid 1960s.

Once many universities—and subsequently much of our public educational system—were overtaken by those not motivated by great scholarship and honest commitment to history and everything was seen from the viewpoint of race, sex, and class, the words "E Pluribus

Unum" ("out of many, one") became increasingly irrelevant. As President Dwight Eisenhower said in his first inaugural address, we become a people that "values its privileges above its principles." And he warned a country that does so "soon loses both." [14]

Eisenhower, in many ways, was echoing our first president, George Washington, who believed deeply in the political and philosophical principles upon which America was founded. In his first inaugural address, he stated, "religion and morality" are the "firmest props of the duties of men and citizens." He added they are the eternal and indispensable pillars supporting "the dispositions and habits which lead to political prosperity." He continued, "[R]eason and experience both forbid us to expect that national morality can prevail in exclusion of religious principle." [15]

Mark David Hall concurs, writing, "Christian ideas underlie some key tenets of America's constitutional order. For instance, the Founders believed that humans are created in the image of God (*imago Dei*), which led them to design institutions and laws meant to protect and promote human dignity." He adds, since they were convinced man is sinful, they tried to avoid the concentration of power by framing the government with carefully enumerated powers. He concludes, "the founders were committed to liberty, but they never imagined that provisions of the Bill of Rights would be used to protect licentiousness. And they clearly thought moral considerations should inform legislation. America has drifted from these first principles. We would do well to reconsider the wisdom of those changes." [16]

Therefore, it is doubly tragic that our schoolchildren and young adult university students are not learning the principles and resulting spiritual foundation that provided the essential glue holding our society together. Without such a fundamental understanding of the American colonists' seeing themselves as the new Israelites and the importance they placed on biblical values, they have no foundation upon which to build character, communities, critical thinking skills, and most of all, purpose in life. Without such purpose, everything is eventually lost.

Additionally, the removal of the guardrails of which Tocqueville spoke has had tragic repercussions, which we will discuss in the chapter on virtue. But the ultimate result was articulated in the following statement by the late American historian (and atheist) Will Durant:

> What happens at a certain point in history is that the intellectual classes abandon the ancient theology, and after some hesitation, the moral code allied with it. Literature and philosophy become anti-clerical. The movement of liberation rises to an exuberant worship of reason and falls to a paralyzing disillusionment with every dogma and every idea. Conduct deprived of its religious support deteriorates into epicurean chaos and life itself shorn of consoling faith becomes a burden alike to conscious poverty and to weary wealth. In the end, a society and its religion tend to fall together like body and soul in a harmonious death.... [17]

Millions of Americans—regardless of if they have faith or no faith at all, like Durant—still strongly agree with the biblical principles our forefathers brought to these shores, even as many other countries with similar foundations—such as Canada and much of Western Europe—have discarded these principles. Many Americans still hold them firmly. These principles must be restored if America is to continue to be a shining city on a hill.

So, how do we restore biblical principles? As we will discuss in succeeding chapters, our nation needs to return to the understanding of the Founders in every aspect of our culture. We must shape the rising generation's hearts and minds to reject the prevailing ideology that says America was established by oppressors and restore the teaching that those who fled to America were seeking freedom and true human flourishing.

It means being sure we have a strong grounding in Christian worldview before we go out to engage the world. One of the best resources we are aware of to equip Christians with the biblical arguments to counter the falsehoods of the world is *The Truth Project*, a video curriculum featuring our mutual friend, Dr. Del Tackett. It is available at http://www.thetruthproject.org/.

To re-instill this knowledge of the biblical values upon which America was established and upon which our nation prospered and thrived is among the most urgent challenges of our time. We have arrived at an hour when the ground is fertile to achieve this goal because we are living in a time when millions of Americans are keenly aware of a great social and moral upheaval. And we need to return to the values upon which our nation was based before it is too late.

These Americans want a better pathway for themselves, their children, and their grandchildren. Finally, these Americans want to restore our great nation's historical and natural affinity for God. They want to live by values derived from the Christian worldview of our nation's Founders, and they want to incorporate these values into their daily lives and into the daily currents of America's public square. From this restoration will flow a reinvigoration and restoration of the Founders' vision for our beloved country. To quote an old Jerome Kern song from the great Fred Astaire–Ginger Rogers musical *Swing Time*, these Americans feel it is time we "pick ourselves up, dust ourselves off, and start all over again."

And, if we do this in every aspect of our culture, we will have the potential to spark a great American renaissance and a future based on hope, instead of fear; love, instead of hate; respect, instead of loathing. The restoration of America—the country Tocqueville knew—will begin.

CHAPTER TWO

Restoring Religious Liberty

"It may be a tragic experience for this country and for its conception of life, liberty, and the pursuit of happiness if our people lose their religious feelings and are left to live their lives without faith. The Constitution does not demand that every friendly gesture between church and state be discountenanced; nor that every vestige of God be eradicated." [1]

—Judge Elbert T. Gallagher

"It is in accordance with their dignity as persons—that is being, endowed with reason and free will and therefore privileged to bear personal responsibility—that all men should at once be impelled by nature and also bound by a moral obligation to seek the truth, especially religious truth. They are also bound to adhere to the truth, once it is known, and to order their lives in accord with the demands of truth. However, men cannot discharge these obligations in a manner in keeping with their own nature unless they enjoy immunity from external coercion as well as psychological freedom. Therefore the right to religious freedom has its foundation not in the subjective disposition of the person, but in his very nature." [2]

—Dignitatis Humanae

"Religious freedom—as the nation has traditionally understood it— can't be a major concern for people who don't respect the importance of religious faith. And human rights, without a grounding in God or some higher moral order, are just a matter of public conscience. They're an act of government largesse, dressed up in pious language about human dignity." [3]

—Archbishop Charles Chaput, Archdiocese of Philadelphia

"Religious liberty might be supposed to mean that everybody is free to discuss religion. In practice it means that hardly anybody is allowed to mention it." [4]

—G. K. Chesterton

Many in America's founding generation knew and experienced firsthand religious persecution. The prevalence of religious persecution in Europe made colonial America a refuge for men and women who faced opposition in their native countries as they sought to practice freely their faith. It is clear early Americans saw this freedom to worship according to conscience—rather than according to the dictates of government—as crucial to human flourishing and to the well-ordered society because they enshrined protections for it in the First Amendment of the U.S. Constitution.

But a sea change happened in 1947 when, in an opinion in the case *Everson v. Board of Education,* former Supreme Court Justice Hugo Black codified a different understanding of the First Amendment.

Everson involved a New Jersey law that allowed the state to reimburse parents who paid to use buses operated by the public transportation system to get their children to and from school at various Catholic institutions. This reimbursement did not promote Catholic doctrine in any way, shape, or form. While the Court ruled the law was not enacted in violation of the U.S. Constitution, in his opinion Justice Black stated, "The First Amendment has erected a wall between church and state. That wall must be kept high and impregnable." [5]

The frequent use of that phrase, "separation of church and state," has convinced millions of Americans—including many people of faith—it is part of either the Constitution or the First Amendment and is a just representation of the Founders' attitude toward religious freedom. Those words are nowhere in the founding documents and, in fact, represent a decided swerve from earlier conceptions of the role of religion in American society.

They are instead from a letter written by one of the Founding Fathers several years after both of those documents were drafted. Nevertheless, they have become a mantra for secularists in every area of American culture to silence people of faith and drive religion from the public square.

The First Amendment casts a vision quite different from this modern understanding of religious freedom. It reads, "Congress shall make no law respecting an establishment of religion, or prohibiting the free exercise thereof; or abridging the freedom of speech, or of the press; or the right of the people to peaceably assemble, and to petition the Government for a redress of grievances."

Judge Elbert T. Gallagher warned about the ramifications of Justice Black's words in 1958 when he dismissed a complaint against an ecumenical committee's attempts to install a Nativity scene on public school property in the village of Ossining, New York. In the dismissal, Judge Gallagher said the concept of the wall of separation between church and state was misleading. He cautioned that if it continued to be used by the courts, the American public would become convinced it was in the Constitution and we would lose sight of the vision of a free and robustly religious public square that so inspired the Founding Fathers. Judge Gallagher's words went unheeded and his prediction has, over time, slowly become true.[6]

Nearly thirty years later, in 1985, Supreme Court Justice William Rehnquist wrote a dissent in *Wallace v. Jaffree* that dealt with the propagation of Justice Black's "wall of separation" error. In *Wallace*, the Supreme Court struck down moments of silence for voluntary prayer or meditation at the beginning of public school days.

Rehnquist wrote it was "impossible to build sound constitutional doctrine upon a mistaken understanding of constitutional history."

He added, the "greatest injury of the 'wall' notion is its mischievous diversion of judges from the actual intentions of the drafters of the Bill of Rights." He concluded, "The 'wall of separation between church and state' is a metaphor based on bad history, a metaphor which has proved useless as a guide to judging. It should be frankly and explicitly abandoned."[7]

Rehnquist was correct. Unfortunately, in the seventy-plus years since Justice Black penned the words "wall of separation between church and state," freedom *of* religion has become confused with freedom *from* religion as groups hostile to religious faith have tried to reinterpret the intentions of our nation's Founding Fathers.

Freedom of religion means people have the right to practice their faith in both their private and public lives and in accordance with the dictates of their conscience. It also means people have the right not to practice any faith if they so choose. Freedom from religion, in the eyes of secularists, means religious faith must be contained within the four walls of a church or someone's home, and religion has no role in the nation's civil discourse or public policy.

Unfortunately, for the past seven decades, those who have adopted this distortion have gone on the offensive to progressively scrub our nation of any religious influence, as well as attack the right of Americans to live out and practice their faith in businesses, schools, and ultimately their homes and places of worship. While religious freedom still exists and is respected by most Americans, the ability to openly live out that faith continues to be squeezed as it is increasingly challenged in all aspects of our culture.

What the framers of the Constitution intended was to make it impossible for the federal government—in particular, Congress—to establish a national church like the Church of England, or to force sectarian policy on an individual state or the nation as a whole. They did not intend, as Justice Black would have it, for the government to censor public religious expression, deny churches and religious organizations equal access to public facilities, and prohibit churches and government from working together for the good of citizens. Nor did they intend—as has most recently been argued—to require people of faith to censor or abandon their own sincerely held beliefs once they enter the public square.

The gap between the language in the Constitution and the attitude in Justice Black's opinion is so wide it is worth asking just where he came up with the phrase, "wall of separation between church and state," since it is found nowhere in the Constitution.

The words used by Justice Black came from an 1802 letter written by President-elect Thomas Jefferson to the Baptists of Danbury, Connecticut, who were a minority religious group in their commonwealth. During the debate over the language of the First Amendment, Jefferson was serving as ambassador to France and was not living in the United States, so his input into the discussion was severely limited. When he served as governor of Virginia, Jefferson assisted the Baptists in their effort to prohibit the commonwealth from funding the Anglican Church in Virginia. The Danbury Baptists were deeply concerned because Connecticut had established the Congregationalist church as the official state church.

Now that Jefferson was to become the president of the United States, and because of the assistance he offered to the Virginia Baptists, the Danbury Baptists wanted a guarantee that he—and by extension, the federal government—would not establish a national church and not interfere with their ability to express their faith in their own way. In his reply to their letter, Jefferson expressed sympathy with their concerns and assured them in no uncertain terms that he would not allow the federal government to establish an official church and would not deny the Danbury Baptists or others their free exercise of religion. He wrote:

Believing with you that religion is a matter which lies solely between Man and his God; that he owes account to none other for his faith or his worship; that the legitimate powers of government reach actions only and not opinions; I contemplate with sovereign reverence that act of the whole American people which declared that their legislature should "make no law respecting an establishment of religion or prohibiting the free exercise thereof," thus building a wall of separation between Church and State.[8]

In the words of Daniel Dreisbach, a professor of constitutional law and history at American University, Jefferson's words were "a political statement…carefully crafted to reassure Jefferson's Baptist constituents in New England of his continuing commitment to religious rights… [Jefferson's wall] wasn't meant to bar religion from public life but to prevent faith from being either politicized or tread upon by the government."[9]

This historical perspective on Jefferson's letter makes it clear Justice Black seriously misinterpreted the implications of the phrase "wall of separation." Jefferson's record as president supports Dreisbach's argument, as he endorsed many policies that go directly against Justice Black's idea of "separation of church and state" and would anger the secularists of today, including policies allowing congregations to use federal funds to construct churches and dedicating federal funds to supporting missionaries who worked among Native Americans.

The present struggle over religious freedom boils down to two sides. The first believe they have a fundamental right protected by the First Amendment to practice their faith freely and openly in society. The second believe religious freedom is not a fundamental right, and any mention or practice of faith in the public square is a dangerous conflation of church and state. The result is that any public displays of faith by an individual or a community—prayers by elected officials, religious content in public schools, and many other expressions of religious conviction—are now under attack.

The battle shifts from issue to issue. For example, in *Wallace v. Jaffree*, the question was primarily about prayer and religious expression in public schools. In other instances, defenders of the sanctity of life have encountered opposition in the form of laws prohibiting prayer outside abortion clinics.

One of the major flashpoints in the ongoing debate over religious freedom occurred with the Obama administration's Department of Health and Human Services Obamacare mandate. This mandate required employers—even ones with faith-based objections to birth control and abortion—to provide employees with insurance coverage for sterilization procedures and for contraceptives, including contraceptives that cause abortion by preventing embryos from implanting in the uterus.

Many Christian employers objected to the mandate, including a group of Catholic nuns: the Little Sisters of the Poor. Rather than provide a way for employers to opt out of the mandate's requirements if those requirements conflicted with their sincerely held beliefs, the Obama administration dug in its heels. With the support of groups like the ACLU, the administration made it clear to religious and pro-life employers—including the Little Sisters of the Poor—that they must comply with the mandate, even though it was a direct violation of their most deeply held moral beliefs.

If employers chose not to provide access to these abortion-inducing drugs, they faced crippling fines. The scope of the fines involved left these employers, faith-based for-profit businesses, and non-profits like the Little Sisters of the Poor, a difficult choice: comply with the mandate, close their doors, or stand up for their rights. Thankfully, they chose to stand.

The Catholic Church has left an indelible mark on modern health care in the United States. Its core belief in the sacred dignity of every person is underscored by its commitment to making high-quality health care accessible to all, including low-income and rural communities. This same belief in the dignity of all human life also dictates which procedures Catholic hospitals and health care workers cannot provide.

The assault on Catholic health care providers is especially tragic because many small communities would have no access to hospital care if were not for Catholic hospitals.

Thus, the loss of Catholic health care would be at the expense of countless of America's most vulnerable citizens. For instance, the Catholic Health Association reports that in 2016, one out of every six patients were cared for in a Catholic hospital. In 2015, Catholic hospitals handled more than 109 million outpatient visits, twenty million emergency room visits, 529,000 births, and five million hospital admissions.[10]

Writing in *National Review,* Alexandra DeSanctis said these attacks were not so much evidence of "how the Church is harming Americans," but more indicative of the antagonism toward the Church and its distinct morality. She writes, "Left by the wayside is the liberal vision of a civil society as a patchwork quilt, flourishing as a result of distinctive institutions, not in spite of them." [11] Thus, by engaging in such attacks, progressive groups are violating the very liberal principles they profess to believe.

Echoing these comments was David French, who states that these attacks on faith are also an attack on the virtue of believers. In his view, a healthy society would cherish the role the Catholic Church, evangelical ministries, and other religious organizations play in the health care and adoption fields. Unfortunately, the attitude of progressives is this: "Dear Christians, thank you for feeding, housing, and caring for the poor, but unless you do it in the manner we prefer—even to the point of adopting the personnel policies we demand—we will use all the power of law and public shame to bring you into compliance." [12]

He adds that, tragically, the result will be that all the good faith-based groups do to minister to the spiritual and physical needs of millions of Americans will go by the wayside. He also says this is how progressive organizations justify causing faith-based hospitals to close, denying the poorest Americans access to health care.[13] Ideology trumps compassion.

This aggressive approach represents a significant change in direction for progressive groups, which for a long time tried to at least appear supportive of the First Amendment right to religious freedom. Michael Barone, who is not a believer, understands this issue, as well. He writes that progressives have decided it is less important for them that people say what they think and more important that they say what the government requires—which increasingly is to compromise their core beliefs.[14]

In the early 1990s, Nadine Strossen, the president of the American Civil Liberties Union (ACLU) at the time, testified before Congress about how foundational she believed the Religious Freedom Restoration Act (RFRA) to be in the overall landscape of First Amendment protections.

RFRA was introduced in response to the Supreme Court's decision in *Smith v. Employment Division of Oregon*, known also as the "peyote" decision. In this decision, the court held that Oregon could deny unemployment benefits to a person fired for violating a state prohibition on the use of the hallucinogenic drug peyote—even though the use of the drug was part of a Native American religious ritual.

The opinion was based on the idea of the "compelling interest test." In constitutional law, a compelling interest test is a method for determining the constitutionality of a statute that restricts the practice of a fundamental right or distinguishes between people on the basis of a suspect classification. The late Justice Antonin Scalia—normally a strong proponent of religious freedom—wrote in his opinion that the Free Exercise Clause protects religious beliefs, but it does not insulate religiously motivated actions from laws unless the laws single out religion for disfavored treatment. Therefore, the state of Oregon could deny the employment benefits based on the peyote use.

Following this decision, Strossen told Congress RFRA was needed to "restore to religious liberty the same kind of protection that the Court has given and still does give to other fundamental freedoms... [and] ... in order for government to infringe on a liberty, including religious liberty, it has to show that the measure is narrowly tailored so as to do as little damage as possible." [15]

She then proceeded to list those entities and institutions worthy of protection, a list including hospitals and schools with a distinct and particular religious foundation—institutions that today face legal attacks by progressive groups for their beliefs. Strossen told Congress, "these were decisions... that society had previously assumed that religious groups had the right to make for themselves and could not be compelled to change just because society thought otherwise." [16]

Her testimony calling for religious freedom to be afforded the same protections as all other essential liberties described precisely the model our nation needs to re-adopt in order to restore the constitutional precepts of religious liberty.

The RFRA law, which ended up passing, gives equal legal protection to all religious individuals—whether they are Christians, Sikhs, Muslims, Apache Indians, Jews, or part of some other religious tradition. This is how it should be in a pluralistic society. But the situation changed in the early 2000s when RFRA began to be applied to extend legal protections for Christian artists, civil servants, business owners, colleges, and ministries who were being asked to give up their beliefs in favor of causes championed by progressives.

When the Supreme Court ruled in *Burwell v. Hobby Lobby Stores* and *Conestoga Wood Specialties v. Burwell* that under RFRA closely held family businesses could not be forced to comply with the HHS Obamacare mandate, progressive groups let out a collective howl of protest. They immediately launched an assault on not only the federal RFRA, but state RFRA laws, as well. These groups did the same when two years later, the court—in cases involving non-profit organizations such as Little Sisters of the Poor, as well as several Christian colleges— remanded the decision back to the lower courts with the mandate to find a solution that protected these organizations' religious freedom.

But the government is not the only threat to religious freedom. As David French has written in *National Review*, the ultimate threat to religious freedom is not from the government, but from the media. He says a combination of media and cultural pressure slowly bends church and other religious institutions until, in his words, "they buckle, and sacrifice their beliefs." [17] He adds, "once the media pressure sets in, the next reality emerges, American churches and religious institutions are often laden with members who don't share Bible-based doctrinal beliefs."

French also asserts that another part of the problem is that millions of people profess to be Christians, but pick and choose which doctrines they want to follow and those they do not based on cultural trends. This has become known as "cafeteria Christianity." The world sees this inconsistency and figures if these principles are not important to people who call themselves Christians, then why shouldn't Christians bow to the secular worldview? French writes, "To use an analogy, it's almost like some folks believe a religious worldview is like a Jenga tower—you can pull out a few planks without causing the whole edifice to collapse." [18]

French's point is that unless the faithful have the moral courage to stand strong against pressures from inside their churches or schools to conform to the world, religious freedom will remain under attack and ultimately be further circumscribed.

His most compelling (and applicable) point to us as believers is that we cannot expect to get all the benefits of Christian community while cherry-picking what doctrines we want or do not want to follow based on what the culture is dictating at the moment. He writes that it will not work because Christian community and service cannot be separated from the entirety of the Christian faith that compels such community and service. He concludes, "Carve out the doctrines that conflict with modern morals and you gut the faith. When you gut the faith, you ultimately gut the church." [19]

If we are to restore religious liberty, we must engage. We must be involved. This is a time for a historic flood tide of faithful men and women to get involved in the media, in culture, and in public policy debates at the local, state, regional, and national levels. But in doing so, we cannot compromise the core beliefs of our faith if we are to successfully restore America's spiritual foundation and God-given freedoms.

Thus, faithful Americans must continue to be "salt and light" and stand firm for our faith—no matter the costs—in all aspects of the culture if we are to turn back the tide against our most fundamental freedom: religious liberty. As French points out, that means being "salt and light" and standing strong for religious liberty in our little platoons, such as churches and schools. In the following chapters, we will discuss ways we can do just that, because ultimately it is religious faith that will bring about America's restoration.

But we must stand together. This means all of us—regardless of our faith background—who care deeply about the future of religious liberty. We must put our differences aside and join in this battle with those of other faith traditions. Much like the way Catholics and

Evangelicals began a historic cooperation in the late 1980s and early 1990s, now we must begin to deepen our cooperation and work with conservative and Orthodox Jews, Muslims, Sikhs, Mormons, and those of other minority faiths who face the same threats.

In this cooperation, we must demonstrate the progressive Left has not merely assaulted the rights of a particular group—evangelical Christians and Catholics—but has arrayed itself against a set of constitutional rights fundamental to being human.

Daniel Mark, an assistant professor of political science at Villanova University and an Orthodox Jew, understands this. He writes that religious freedom is under attack because traditional beliefs are a threat to radical autonomy. Thus, the entire idea of human rights has been assaulted because liberty has become confused with license. They are two different concepts. License means being free to do whatever you want, which is anarchy. Liberty means we are free to pursue what we believe in our hearts is good.

Mark concludes, "In these circumstances, we need to discover—or recover—a proper account of rights. This begins with a proper grasp of the good of religion, and finally, all the goods that constitute human flourishing." [20]

If humans are to flourish—and, in turn, America is to flourish—the road to renewal starts here. The restoration of our constitutionally protected right of religious liberty and conscience has never been more urgent or timely than it is now. The questions we must all ask ourselves are these: "What will I do to defend these freedoms for future generations?" and "How can I treat those who may oppose my values with dignity and respect?" Our answer to those questions will have an eternal impact.

CHAPTER THREE

Restoring Medicine and Medical Ethics

*"Nearly four thousand years of Judeo-Christian tradition taught us that
every human life is sacred and has inviolable dignity. Reason alone tells
us that human life is special and we have a duty to protect one another.
And that duty is especially strong when dealing with those in a weakened
and vulnerable state. Once we abandon these values—once our society
accepts a hierarchy or pecking order of human life—all of the rights and
protections that follow from these luminous principles are lost."* [1]

**—Dr. Philip Hawley, hospice physician and former assistant
professor of clinical pediatrics at University of
Southern California Keck School of Medicine**

*"I swear to fulfill, to the best of my ability and judgment, this covenant:
I will respect the hard-won scientific gains of those physicians in whose
steps I walk, and gladly share such knowledge as is mine with those who
are to follow.*

*"I will apply, for the benefit of the sick, all measures [that] are required,
avoiding those twin traps of overtreatment and therapeutic nihilism.*

*"I will remember that there is art to medicine as well as science, and
that warmth, sympathy, and understanding may outweigh the surgeon's
knife or the chemist's drug.*

*"I will not be ashamed to say 'I know not,' nor will I fail to call in my
colleagues when the skills of another are needed for a patient's recovery.*

*"I will respect the privacy of my patients, for their problems are not
disclosed to me that the world may know. Most especially must I tread
with care in matters of life and death. If it is given me to save a life, all
thanks. But it may also be within my power to take a life; this awesome*

*responsibility must be faced with great humbleness and awareness of
my own frailty. Above all, I must not play at God.*

*"I will remember that I do not treat a fever chart, a cancerous growth,
but a sick human being, whose illness may affect the person's family and
economic stability. My responsibility includes these related problems, if
I am to care adequately for the sick.*

*"I will prevent disease whenever I can, for prevention is
preferable to cure.*

*"I will remember that I remain a member of society, with special obli-
gations to all my fellow human beings, those sound of mind and body
as well as the infirm.*

*"If I do not violate this oath, may I enjoy life and art, respected while I
live and remembered with affection thereafter. May I always act so as
to preserve the finest traditions of my calling and may I long experience
the joy of healing those who seek my help."* [2]

– The modern-day Hippocratic oath

A while back, Tim spoke to a classroom of Georgetown University undergraduate students on the topic of faith and public
life. While he had been to Georgetown on a number of other
occasions, this time the class was, in his view, electric. The professor
was brilliant, and the students not only asked probing questions that
showed they were fully engaged in the topic, but also were insightful
in their observations.

As he closed his remarks, Tim noted that for the next speaker, the
class ought to think about inviting someone who specialized in the
relationship between faith and medicine, that is, bioethics. Bioethics
is a branch of academic study that purposely seeks out the difficult
issues of life and death—often under the most trying circumstances—
and works to both acknowledge and then deal with the ways in which

civilized societies work through the practical and difficult issues of the sick and dying.

With the dawning of the twenty-first century and the resulting rapid advancements in medical science, Tim suggested to the students that the relationship between Christian faith and these advances was more complex and perplexing than at any other time in human history.

When Tim made this comment, a young woman sitting in the front row retorted, "Faith and politics, okay. But please, not a lecture on faith and medicine. They don't go together."

To this day, Tim regrets not staying to talk further with the student about that comment. On his drive back to the office, Tim kept asking himself what she could have meant by it. It slowly became obvious as he traversed the D.C. traffic that she firmly believed speaking with conviction about how one's faith merges with his or her practice of medicine was a bridge too far to contemplate.

Tim also realized he had always assumed high school and college science classes included ethics discussions. But the student's comment forced him to reconsider that assumption. Was it possible American students were simply not being asked to consider the relationship between science and ethics, let alone science and faith?

We live in day of rapid medical advancements that, on one side of the equation, allow people to live longer and more fulfilled lives. This is a wonderful thing. However, these advancements also have a dark side with legalized abortion and physician-assisted suicide, which make it easier to take life prematurely at its beginning and near its end. Added to that are issues such as human cloning, where man is seeking to replace God as the author and creator of life. And the result is a thorny thicket of issues with which the faithful healthcare professional who believes in *imago Dei*—that all men are made in the image of God—must wrestle.

Several years ago, during Craig's annual wellness visit, his doctor mentioned a dilemma he had faced the day before. The doctor, a committed Christian, had a teenage patient come to him with one goal: to receive a referral for an abortion. The doctor explained as kindly as he could that he could not give her the referral, as he could not participate in any way in the taking of an innocent human life.

The teenage girl stalked out of his office, angry that she did not get what she wanted. She immediately went on Yelp and gave this highly competent and respected doctor a scathing review. While her words were upsetting to him and he was saddened to see his professional reputation unfairly attacked, this doctor knew he did the right thing. Conviction made it possible for him to have peace about his decision—even knowing the review could adversely affect his practice.

Unfortunately, many health professionals face ongoing pressure to violate deeply held beliefs about the sanctity of human life.

Bioethicist Wesley Smith, senior fellow at the Discovery Institute's Center on Human Exceptionalism, writes, "The medical and bioethics establishments and the international abortion lobby want to drive pro-life and Hippocratic Oath–believing doctors, midwives, and nurses out of medicine." He adds the authoritarian tactic being used to accomplish this is to wipe out medical conscience—the civil right to choose not to participate in legal medical procedures when an individual has a religious or moral objection to them.[3]

Smith goes on to cite international examples of this, such as a law in Victoria, Australia, requiring doctors who are unwilling to perform an abortion to provide support nevertheless through procuring an abortionist for the patient—the dilemma Craig's doctor faced.

He also cites another law in Ontario, Canada, involving assisted suicide, which requires physicians to perform euthanasia or refer someone to a doctor who will—a law upheld by a Canadian court that acknowledged it violated the physicians' rights under the Canadian Charter of Freedoms to "freedom of conscience and religion."[4]

According to a report titled "Unconscionable: When Providers Deny Abortion Care," abortion and euthanasia advocates should require those who object "to justify their positions and to perform an alternative service." It continues, "Similarly, they should assume responsibility for the burdens caused by their refusal to provide services for their patients, their peers, and the health care system by providing adequate and timely information and referrals to women, and by performing extra duties to relieve their non-objecting colleagues."[5]

Smith concludes:

> The drive to destroy medical conscience seeks to transform abortion into a positive right, which would require the state to guarantee access. The only effective way to that is to coerce doctors to do the deed … the struggle over medical conscience will ultimately determine whether doctors, nurses, midwives, and pharmacists will retain their freedom, or be required by law to hew to secular progressive values as the moral price of obtaining—or keeping—a professional license.[6]

Several years after his lecture at Georgetown University, Tim spoke with a young woman in St. Louis who shared that for her entire life she had aspired and worked to become a nurse in a major urban hospital so she could treat the whole person—medically, emotionally, holistically, and spiritually.

After years of hard work, she finally achieved her goal, but just days before starting her new job, her manager told her under no circumstances could she ever discuss her faith with patients or their families.

In other words, this young woman learned she would not be allowed to bring her whole self—with all of her passions and convictions—to her job. Part of herself, possibly her very core, had to stay at home. The very motivation—to be Christ to her patients—that inspired her to work so hard and to pursue her career was being taken away to be replaced by a clinical mentality that did not take the welfare of the whole person into account.

The truth is, in America today, health care professionals like this young nurse in St. Louis are being told when they enter their profession that they must check their faith at the door. But that does not need to be the case.

So how can faith and the practice of health care be reconciled? As Tim thought more and more about this relationship, his mind took him back to Georgetown University and to Dr. Edmund Pellegrino, considered to be one of the founders of bioethics.

From 2005–2009, Pellegrino served on the President's Council on Bioethics. Before this appointment, he served as the director of Georgetown University's Kennedy Institute of Ethics and as the founder of the Center for Clinical Bioethics there, which was renamed in his honor. Pellegrino authored more than six hundred published articles and chapters in medical science, philosophy, and ethics. He also authored or co-authored twenty-three books, and his research interests included the history of medicine, the philosophy of medicine, professional ethics, the patient-physician relationship, and biomedical ethics in a culturally pluralistic society.

Pellegrino previously served as the president of the Yale University-New Haven Medical Center. It was there he began teaching some of the first medical school courses in bioethics in the country. Thanks in part to his efforts, every major medical school in America has an ethics requirement for its graduates.

Pellegrino summed up his view on bioethics best when he said, "Medicine is a moral enterprise and if you take away the ethical and moral dimensions, you end up with a technique. The reason it's a profession is that it's dedicated to something other than its own self-interests."[7]

From that statement, it is clear Pellegrino knew ethics, rooted in faith, must be part of a physician's training. Otherwise, the doctor has no purpose and there is little to differentiate him or her from an automobile mechanic who replaces or repairs aging parts. He recalled that when he was in medical school at New York University in the 1940s, a typical ethics requirement took about two hours. There was no specific course. To him, that was not acceptable. There was no way a physician could learn how to make informed decisions about life and death in the amount of time it takes to watch a movie, so he pioneered a better way forward born of his moral imagination.

Pellegrino was unique and indispensable in the field because he was both a doctor and a philosopher. As mentioned earlier, he wrote or co-wrote numerous books and articles that looked at the deeper issues beyond just medicine. As such, his research demonstrates an ongoing passion for exploring the ethical and philosophical dimensions of health care in an era when medical professionals acquired the ability to lengthen or shorten human life through science in a manner unparalleled in history to date.

When he passed away in 2013 at the age of ninety-two, he left a legacy of a sixty-seven-year marriage to his wife, Clementine, seven children, two grandchildren, and a great-grandson as a testament to the circle of life. His path-breaking book *A Philosophical Basis of Medical Practice* will continue to be read and studied for years to come, as its words are derived from the pen of a man with a fertile mind and spirit. His was a life well-lived.

Upon Pellegrino's passing, Maggie Little, the current director of Georgetown's Kennedy Institute of Ethics, said, "Those who know his work know he was an icon of bioethics. Those who had a chance to talk with him will know he was also one of the most humble and kindest of men." Dr. G. Kevin Donovan, director of the renamed Edmund D. Pellegrino Center for Clinical Bioethics and a pediatrics professor at Georgetown University Medical Center, said, "As a founding father of modern bioethics, he has had an immense effect on students, residents, and practicing physicians. He taught virtue ethics and personified it in his actions. He always recalled our attention to the bedrock of medical practice, the primacy of the doctor-patient relationship."

Yet for all his achievements in academia, Pellegrino was not simply a philosopher with his head in the clouds. What fascinated him was the point at which ideas and theories impacted specific, real-life medical situations. He was a clinician at heart, but he understood the reality of decisions being made in the clinic, tracing their roots to the university, the classroom, the philosophical discussion about human life and its value, and ultimately to the metaphysical convictions in the doctor's soul.

He once told a student, "In a philosophy class, you can argue, 'On the one hand, this, on the other, that.' In medicine, you've got to take a position. And there are always conflicts, conflicts of obligations. You've got to resolve them. That's what medical ethics is all about." [8]

While the idea of medical ethics goes back to Hippocrates, it was Pellegrino who insisted upon a firm foundation upon which those ethics must be built. He knew ethics built on shaky metaphysical ground could lead to horrific consequences—consider, for example, the career of Dr. Josef Mengele in Nazi Germany. Mengele's skill as a doctor and his grasp of the scientific principles behind medicine were objectively quite sound, but his ethical system was based on a fundamentally evil metaphysical conviction that history was moving inexorably toward producing a "master race."

This meant Mengele's ethics, like those of his fellow Nazi leaders, often assumed "Might makes right" and "The end justifies the means"—the end being the elevation of the German race above all others. This corrupt framework gave Mengele the rational basis for using his scientific skill not to promote life, but to conduct unthinkable experiments on living people, develop new and chilling methods of torture, and condemn countless men, women, and children to the gas chambers and ovens.[9]

As his earlier statement attests, Pellegrino understood ethics cannot stand alone; it must be connected to something deeper. For him—as for many healthcare professionals, such as Craig's doctor—that "something deeper" is Christian faith and Christ's mandate to "Love thy neighbor."

Pellegrino knew it would be impossible for him to construct one ethical system to apply to medicine and one to apply to the rest of his life; no human person can bifurcate himself or herself that way without doing serious damage to his conscience and psyche. He also knew from the example of the grievous events of the twentieth century—such as those of Nazi Germany—the importance of finding a solid foundation for ethics. Pellegrino became convinced it was his professional duty to weave his Christian faith into his work as a doctor—not to try to lay it aside. His faith, he came to believe, was far from peripheral to his work as a doctor. It was a central component that enabled him to use his God-given skills for good and not be seduced into betraying his Creator by succumbing to the temptation to use them to promote unjust and inhumane ideologies.

Pellegrino saw no inherent inconsistency between faith and reason. In fact, the two are mutually beneficial in the search for truth. He believed, along with the vast majority of Christian thinkers throughout history, the ability to reason was also a God-given gift—one that can enhance and deepen our faith and our knowledge of God.

He was convinced that faith, combined with reason, allowed Christians to formulate principles that gave them guidelines for how to act in specific situation. In other words, he believed faith and reason together led directly to the formation of an ethical system. It was this ethical system, composed of faith-based convictions and rational conclusions from those convictions, which Pellegrino relied upon when he faced major medical decisions in real-life situations.

Pellegrino, as his colleagues attested, believed that the doctor-patient relationship was foundational and unbreakable. He loved being with his patients and with their families when the tough decisions had to be made. The sanctity of all human life, no matter what stage from birth to natural death, guided him in the way he practiced medicine. He never forgot the idea of the soul. In his words, a physician, "binds himself to competence as a moral obligation [placing] the well-being of those he presumes to help above his own personal gain." [10]

Pellegrino's most noteworthy achievement and legacy from his service on the President's Council of Bioethics was his relentless insistence on including theologians in the mix of making major life-and-death medical decisions. He personally ensured the views of Christian health care professionals were not sidelined, either when lawyers and social scientists discussed medical policies at the highest levels or when patients and their families faced critical decisions about life and death.

Finally, he saw the value and utility of the eternal truth that all life is sacred and all men are made *imago Dei*, and he welcomed them into the most difficult decisions concerning life and death. Pellegrino made it clear that he opposed abortion,[11] euthanasia, and physician-assisted suicide[12] because he believed the taking of innocent human life was a violation of the Hippocratic oath to "first do not harm." [13] His interpretation of that oath—like everything else in his life—was rooted first and foremost in his Christian faith, which attributed great dignity to every human life because of each life's participation in the *imago Dei*.

As the field of medical philosophy continues to grow, one of the great questions now before us is whether Christianity will continue to have a central voice in it. Pellegrino showed that our faith in Jesus Christ can and should play a leading role in the largest ethical debates of our times where the very nature of what it means to be a person is at the core of the discussion—human cloning, abortion, genetic engineering, gene editing, and artificial intelligence, to name just a few.

Another leading ethicist, Dr. Phillip Hawley, a hospice physician and former assistant professor of clinical pediatrics at the University of Southern California Keck School of Medicine, concurs. He writes, "If human life has innate dignity and value, if human life comprises universal goods that we must promote and defend, then physicians have a duty to protect every human life." [14]

But unfortunately, modern medicine often does the opposite. Hawley has also written that the "inconsistency of modern bioethics is breathtaking." He states:

> On the one hand, if you want to end your chronic suffering or deal with a terminal illness by committing suicide, today's utilitarian ethicists will invoke personal autonomy as the guiding principle and endorse your plans. But if you choose to continue living in spite of your suffering or terminal diagnosis, those same ethicists brush aside the notion of personal autonomy, label your request as unreasonable, and conclude that you are sadly incapable of making the "right" choice. [15]

New York University philosophy teacher Gerald T. Mundy, writing in the *Public Discourse*, lays out arguments for why it is incongruent for someone who has sworn an oath to protect life to participate actively in the taking of life. He writes that a good doctor will seek to achieve health and longevity of the patient, instead of trying to hasten death. He adds that a physician cannot truly and wholeheartedly work toward restoring the health of his patient if they know they can simply give up at any time and recommend that the patient choose death, instead of life.

He concludes:

> The psychological effect of knowing there is an option of suggesting assisted suicide when treatment becomes difficult will affect even the most disciplined physician. For the physician will always know, when faced with a patient who is difficult to treat or to cure, that there is another choice available. If he is willing to use the assisted suicide option, he *cannot* be devoted fully to his patient's life. Physicians who are *truly* opposed to this choice of ends are the ones who save lives.[16]

Pellegrino was one of those doctors. He wrote, "The capacity to make moral judgments, and to be self-critical, is part of being an educated person. That's what I do with ethics. I don't set out to make trouble, but, when I do cause a stir, it's only because I raise questions that strike me as unavoidable." [17]

When it comes to matters of life and death, these questions are certainly unavoidable for us all. Pellegrino gave us all a model to follow. As doctors swear an oath to "do no harm," we as society must do so, as well, and affirm that all life is made *imago Dei* and should be treated with the utmost dignity and respect, which will be the focus of our next chapter.

CHAPTER FOUR

Restoring a Culture of Life

"The Gospel of life is at the heart of Jesus's message. Lovingly received day after day by the Church, it is to be preached with dauntless fidelity as 'good news' to the people of every age and culture." [1]
—**Saint John Paul II,** *Evangelium Vitae*, 1995

M arch 21 is World Down Syndrome Day. It is a day to celebrate and affirm the precious lives of these special-needs
children made in the *imago Dei*, each having inherent
dignity. Despite the special challenges these children can present to
their families, most parents love and cherish them regardless of their
condition.

However, two months earlier, there is a day that not only does not
celebrate these lives, but in fact puts them and millions of others in
deadly peril.

January 22 is the day the United States Supreme Court, in 1973,
issued perhaps its most controversial decision ever: *Roe v. Wade.* This
decision overturned abortion laws in all fifty states, forcing states to
allow abortion on demand right up to the moment of live birth. Since
the issuance of this outrageous decision, more than sixty million innocent children have lost the chance to live their lives. [2] And sadly, some

parents, if they discover their child will have Down syndrome, are openly encouraged to abort their child rather than deal with such a burden or "inconvenience." Presently, it is estimated that 67–90 percent of all babies in the United States with Down syndrome are aborted. In England, the rate is 90 percent, and in Iceland, it is 100 percent.[3]

The same sad scenario is true with other children with developmental disabilities. The premature deaths of those lost lives represent a staggering loss of human potential, creativity, and flourishing for America as a whole. But the ramifications of *Roe v. Wade* are even greater. The Supreme Court's decision fundamentally altered the way human life is treated in the American legal system. Instead of seeing each life—born or pre-born—as representing the *imago Dei*, human life within the womb is now considered under the law a commodity to be disposed of whenever it is deemed inconvenient.

It has not taken long for this philosophy of convenience to spread outward and encompass life at all stages—not just the lives of the unborn.

In Europe—and even in multiple states throughout America— many ethicists, politicians, philosophers, and even doctors assert that those at the end of life now have a "duty to die" rather than live and be a "burden" on their children and community. Princeton University ethicist Peter Singer has long been famous for advocating for the moral duty to "weed out" what he says is inconvenient life—a category he believes includes the sick, the unborn, the elderly, and special needs individuals.[4]

In March 2018 in the widely read publication the *Washington Post*, deputy editorial page director Ruth Marcus wrote that special needs children, such as those with Down syndrome, are "undesirables" who can and should be eliminated to suit the preferences of others in society.[5] She asserted that if her preborn child was diagnosed with Down syndrome, she would gladly abort it because "that was not the child I wanted." [6] Such language brings back ugly memories of Nazi Germany, where scientists and eugenicists crafted large-scale systems to sterilize, purge, and eliminate all people who did not fit the mold of the idealized "master race."

The basis for these arguments is a simple philosophical principle: *the ultimate purpose of life is self-fulfillment*, or determining your own destiny.

This denial of *imago Dei* and the elevation of "self-fulfillment" above all else lead to inevitable and tragic conclusions, such as the justification of taking innocent lives perceived to be less than perfect or who were conceived in circumstances or at times that might otherwise be perceived as inconvenient. Human beings want life on their terms—not God's terms.

This is where the issue of medical ethics, which we discussed in the last chapter, and the sanctity of human life come together. Without a set of ethics based on the *imago Dei*, evil flourishes—such as eugenics, euthanasia, abortion, and infanticide. An example of this is found in parts of Europe, such as Belgium and the Netherlands, where the killing of "burdensome" human life—including the killing of small children—is now legally sanctioned. [7]

Once *imago Dei* is abandoned and man no longer sees himself in the image of God, but living only for his own self-fulfillment, he becomes merely another mammal. This mindset was probably best expressed by Ingrid Newkirk, the founder of People for the Ethical Treatment of Animals (PETA), when she asserted that "a rat is a pig is a dog is a boy." [8]

This disregard for life is not a new thing. In 1915, America learned of the case of the "Bollinger Baby" in which a doctor chose to allow an infant to die rather than perform the surgery that would have saved the child's life. The baby boy was paralyzed on the left side of his body and was missing his left ear altogether and the eardrum of his right ear. His right cheek was connected to his shoulder and he had a curved spine and closure of the intestinal tract.[9] All of these things were correctable. The doctor, Harry J. Haiselden, later admitted he had allowed the death of other "defective babies."[10]

At about the same time, Margaret Sanger founded the American Birth Control League, which would eventually be re-branded as Planned Parenthood. In her autobiography, Sanger admitted she founded Planned Parenthood in order "to stop the multiplication of the unfit." She believed this was "the most important and greatest step towards race betterment."[11]

In order to make her overt disdain for human life politically palatable, Sanger cloaked her deadly agenda under the cause of women's health. Her real agenda was not women's health, but eugenics and blatant racism.

She recommended that abortionists kill "defective" children to create "a new breed of thoroughbreds" while advocating for "birth control" bureaus that would engage in the "science of breeding." She called those whom she saw as inferior as "those human weeds which threaten the blooming of the finest flowers of American civilization."[12] In a 1957 interview with the late CBS reporter Mike Wallace, she stated that she believed children she deemed to be less than desirable or perfect should be discarded—calling it the "greatest sin" to bring what she deemed to be "unfit" children from "unfit" parents in the world.[13]

Sanger also had little regard for freedom of conscience for people of faith who believe in the *imago Dei*. In the same interview, she told Wallace that Catholics could not legally protest or stop the use of their tax dollars to subsidize birth control.[14]

In 2012, the Obama administration attempted via its Department of Health and Human Services (HHS) mandate to force ministries, faith-based colleges, and family-owned businesses to provide free access to abortion-inducing drugs or face crippling fines. The administration's actions were in line with Sanger's statement from more than fifty years earlier: people of faith had to financially and, in some cases, materially, facilitate the taking of innocent human life.

These ministries, colleges, and family-owned businesses faced punishment for choosing *not* to facilitate ways to make birth control—including those forms demonstrated to lead to early-term abortions—available to their employees. They had to do so *even though* those members and employees were, in large part, not asking for access to the contraceptives, which were also available at a low cost through other sources.

It soon became clear the intention of the mandate was not merely to give women access to contraceptives—it was to force all employers, possibly against their missions and consciences, to provide access to those contraceptives. The result, in effect, was that all businesses and organizations objecting to contraception or abortifacients would have to either give up their convictions or go out of business.

These ministries, colleges, and businesses knew the time had come to take a stand. Although these organizations spent years operating under immediate threat of bankruptcy and extinction because of the HHS mandate about contraception, they filed dozens of lawsuits to block the implementation of the mandate.

Some of those cases gradually made their way up to the U.S. Supreme Court, which upheld the religious freedom of closely held, family-owned businesses. In its decision, the court stated the government could not force these businesses to facilitate the taking of innocent human life. Two years later, the U.S. Supreme Court ordered the federal government and lower courts to find a compromise on the same issue for Christian colleges and ministries.

To restore a culture of life is going to require us to stand for life as these ministries, colleges, and businesses did, often at great personal and professional expense.

Unfortunately, some individuals say they are "personally pro-life" but choose to do nothing to stop the continued killing of innocent human lives. These individuals—including many current lawmakers—are exactly like those throughout history who either stood idly on the sidelines or tried to compromise with, rather than confront, evil. They have chosen personal ambition and comfort over principle.

To restore a culture of life, we need to be more than "personally pro-life." We need to be pro-life in our actions, as well.

NFL star Ben Watson is one such person who has put his pro-life beliefs into action. When the ultrasound machine—a vital tool for pregnancy care centers—at a Selena Park, Maryland, pregnancy center fell into disrepair, Watson generously donated a new, state-of-the-art 3D/4D ultrasound machine. The center operates out of a former abortion clinic that still has bloodstains from the abortions performed there. Watson made the gift through the Ethics and Religious Liberty Commission of the Southern Baptist Church and Focus on the Family's Option Ultrasound Program.

Watson wrote about his gift:

> Years ago, after a 3D/4D ultrasound for our first child, we envisioned the day when we would be able to give families this gift.... For me, as I yawned after seeing my daughter yawn in utero, the pregnancy became real in a much more tangible way.... Seeing life inside the womb not only affirms its beauty and dignity but encourages the mother and father that their child is worth fighting for.[15]

While not everyone has the financial means of an NFL star to provide an ultrasound machine to a pregnancy care center, there are other steps we can take to restore a culture of life in America. Tim's church financially supports the ASSIST Crisis Pregnancy Resource

Center in Northern Virginia, and Craig's church financially and materially supports the With Child Pregnancy Center in Phoenix.

When a faith-based organization, college, or business refuses to provide access to abortion-inducing drugs, we must stand with it. When a health care professional refuses to participate in the taking of an innocent human life, we must stand with him or her. We must stand with pro-life pregnancy centers offering compassionate care to both a mother and the child in her womb and stand against those who seek to shut down their life-saving efforts.

For those women who have made the choice to kill their unborn child, we must reach out to them with love and compassion, and not hatred and condemnation. There are many, many factors that go into this choice—none of which excuse it, but none of which can be ignored as we consider how best to love post-abortive women. While we cannot condone the choice they made, we can share with them—despite that choice—that forgiveness and healing can come through Jesus Christ, who sees their hurt and pain. Post-abortive women need to encounter open arms, not closed hearts.

Finally, we must celebrate all life, regardless of its condition or the unique challenges it may present. This is perhaps the strongest message we can send to refute those who feel life is disposable—especially life that is, in their eyes, less than perfect.

Craig's church does just that. It has opened its doors to all families with special-needs children, providing these children not only with a place where they know they are unconditionally loved and cherished, but also where these families can receive the spiritual and emotional support they need to raise their children while maintaining the proper balance in their lives. Church volunteers provide mothers and fathers of special needs children with "date nights" by offering supervised care for their children. The church provides a special Sunday school for these children so their parents can enjoy the morning worship service and receive the nourishment for their souls they will need as they face the daily challenges of raising a special-needs child.

The church also hosts, along with other churches across the country, an annual "Night to Shine"—a prom for people with special needs that celebrates who they are and how much God loves them, just as they are. It has become a citywide celebration of special needs children with several thousand in attendance.

Daniel Darling, the vice president of communications for the Ethics and Religious Liberty Commission, perhaps put it best when he wrote, "The pro-life movement has the moral vocabulary an unjust world needs, but we must not merely see ourselves as an anti-abortion movement, though we are that. We must see ourselves as the human dignity movement, committed to the idea that every human being has intrinsic value." [16]

He goes on to paint a picture of what this would look like if *Roe v. Wade* were overturned. He writes, "Imagine if the end of *Roe* were not the end of advocacy, but the beginning? What if we saw ourselves, not merely as conservatives or anti-abortion activists, but as people who are always, everywhere advocating for policies that help the most vulnerable flourish?"

He concludes:

> Imagine a new kind of politics where the ethic of human dignity disrupted our political categories, uniting those who see the humanity of the unborn with those who see the humanity of the immigrant, the disabled, the infirm, and the elderly? Imagine a new era of civility where we saw dignity even in our fiercest opponents and worked with whoever is willing to end injustices against the innocent? ... if we re-imagine ourselves as a movement for dignity, the pro-life movement will not merely have a legacy of persistently,

courageously, and eloquently arguing on behalf of the unborn but as the people who opposed assaults on humanity, wherever it is found.[17]

Restoring a culture of life starts this way—seeing each life as *imago Dei*. No matter the condition, every life is to be loved and cherished because it has inherent dignity and is precious in God's sight.

May we be the ones who practice such love and restore a culture of life—one life a time.

CHAPTER FIVE

Restoring Marriage, Family, and Social Capital

"Some have suggested that in today's world, the family has somehow become less important. Well, I can't help thinking just the opposite: that when so much around is whispering the little lie that we should live only for the moment and for ourselves, it's more important than ever to affirm an older and more lasting set of values... the family remains the fundamental unit of American life." [1]

—Ronald Reagan

"Marriage and family life are important means ... because they provide invaluable education in and preparation for the responsibilities of self-governing citizenship. Without this moral education, people are poorer, more dependent, and less equipped to become citizens." [2]

—Scott Yenor, Boise State University

"It is not money, but the family that is the foundation of public life. As it has become weaker, every structure built upon that foundation has become weaker." [3]

—James Q. Wilson, professor of government at Harvard University

"The new wealth in America is familial wealth, and the new poverty, familial poverty." [4]

—Mary Eberstadt, senior research fellow
at the Faith and Reason Institute in Washington, D.C.

"It is up to us to show a fraying culture that marriage is so much more than 'just a piece of paper' or an association of any two or more persons who profess to love each other. It is a sacred union of a man and a woman that confers myriad benefits on the spouses, their children, and society at large—benefits that cannot be replicated by any other relationship. I would go so far as to say a society cannot flourish, or even long survive, without stable marriages at its core." [5]

—Jim Daly, president and CEO of Focus on the Family

I n 1965, at the height of the Johnson administration and its "Great Society" programs that greatly expanded government entitlement programs, former Senator Daniel Patrick Moynihan penned his study *The Negro Family: The Case for National Action*, dubbed the "Moynihan Report."

Moynihan was deeply concerned about African American households trapped in a seemingly endless cycle of poverty and identified what he perceived to be the main contributing factor, writing, "The fundamental problem is family structure. The evidence—not final but powerfully persuasive—is that the [African American] family in the urban ghettos is crumbling." [6]

Moynihan, a classical liberal, had no problems with big government intervention to solve issues. However, he also saw that more was needed than just throwing money at a problem in hopes it would go away. Nonetheless, his fellow liberals believed the solution to the problem Moynihan identified (as well as other issues) was a major, historic expansion of the federal government—a.k.a. "the Great Society."

In fact, the huge infusion of federal spending has led to tragic ramifications for marriage, family, and American society as a whole. The inner cities Moynihan perceived as crumbling in 1965 have completely dissolved into chaos and despair over the succeeding fifty-plus years, with the problems spreading out to rural communities, as well.

The "Great Society" was supposed to eliminate poverty and racial injustice. It included programs such as Medicare, Medicaid, welfare, and federal education funding to address urban decay, medical care, and rural poverty. Huge amounts of federal dollars were spent in hopes it would eliminate these problems and create more opportunity.

While these goals are commendable, as time has shown, the implementation of these solutions has exacerbated the very problems it meant to solve.

At the time Moynihan's report was released, about one-quarter of African American children were living in fatherless homes. Moynihan called it a crisis, and indeed it was. But fifty years later, what Moynihan called a crisis has become an epidemic. As of 2014, more than seventy percent of all African American children are now born out of wedlock—triple the percentage Moynihan reported in the mid-1960s when the Great Society was launched to solve the problem (hopefully) of fatherless children in African American homes.[7]

But this disturbing trend is not isolated to the African American community. It now transcends racial boundaries. In 2014, more than half of Hispanic children were born out of wedlock,[8] as well as one-third of all children born to Caucasian mothers.[9] As recently as 1970, only 15 percent of all American babies were born outside of marriage. The combined rate of all racial groups is now a whopping 40 percent.[10] If there is any sign of light at the end of the tunnel, it is that this figure has leveled off in recent years.

When Moynihan issued his report, he hoped it would begin a serious national conversation about the implications for the American family—and society as a whole—if this trend were not reversed. While an advocate of government, he also realized government could not tuck a child into bed at night. Government could not save a marriage, nor could it heal a broken family. These were primarily cultural, not economic or political, problems.

In fact, there is strong evidence the governmental policies implemented in the mid-1960s have torn gaping holes in our national fabric. The institutions of marriage and family are intrinsically linked to what economists call "social capital." In the *Washington Post*, economist Robert Samuelson defined social capital this way: it is "the ability of people to work and play together—to cooperate and connect with others. The stronger a society's social capital, the less isolated and powerless people feel." He warns that in contemporary America, "our social capital is depleting." [11]

The breakdown of the institutions of marriage and family harms all other relationships, crippling the ability for society to operate smoothly. Boise State Professor Scott Yoder puts it succinctly:

> Scarcely any area of public policy is unaffected by the decline in marriage and family life. Educational attainment of children outside of marriage suffers, the job teachers face is more complicated, and crime is connected with fatherlessness.... As the family declines, the state rises to take its place; as the state rises to take its place, the family declines further. [12]

Manhattan Institute Senior Fellow Jason Riley, writing about the Moynihan Report, found through his research that the Great Society penalized marriage and subsidized single parenting.

Riley observed that between 1890 and 1940 African American marriage rates in the U.S. were higher than those of Caucasians. The poverty rate among African Americans fell by forty percent during the 1940s and 1950s. From 1940 to 1970, the number of African Americans in middle-class professions quadrupled. The homicide rate for African American men fell by 18 percent in the 1940s and by another 22 percent in the 1950s.[13] While things were still difficult for African Americans in the inner cities and they found themselves living in a profoundly unjust society with regard to their civil rights, these statistics provided hope for a better future, as well as showed the importance of marriage in the African American community.

But once the government got involved through the Great Society, the tide turned in the opposite—and tragic—direction. The massive government interventions of the Great Society not only stopped that progress, but largely reversed it. Instead of taking small measures to encourage this progress along, the government decided to rush in and try to solve a crisis that was beginning to solve itself.

In almost all the areas which Riley researched—income, academic achievement, and employment—African American families have either stagnated or gone backward over the past fifty years, despite the more than $22 trillion dollars spent on Great Society programs.[14]

Other negative ramifications have been rising out-of-wedlock births and increased poverty. Four out every five African American children raised by a single mother live at or below the poverty line. However, the situation is dramatically different for married African Americans; the poverty rate for this group is below 10 percent.[15]

Riley wrote that the government paid mothers well to keep fathers out of the home. Unfortunately, "the likelihood of teen pregnancy, drug abuse, dropping out of school, and many other social problems grew dramatically when fathers were absent."[16]

Other statistics bear this out. In 1935, the Aid to Families of Dependent Children program (AFDC) was started. By 1960, only 4 percent of the children getting welfare had a mother who had never been married. The remaining children had mothers who were widows or who were separated from their husbands. By 1996, approximately two-thirds of welfare children had an unmarried mother.[17]

In 2002, the late social scientist James Q. Wilson stated that America's marriage crisis would not be solved "from the top down by government policies, but from the bottom up by personal decisions."[18] He explained how money exacerbated the problem, writing, "If a welfare system pays unmarried mothers enough to have their own apartment, some women will prefer babies to husbands. When government subsidizes something, we get more of it."[19]

Economist Mark Rosenzweig verified this. He discovered from the National Longitudinal Survey of Youth that a 10 percent increase in welfare benefits made the chances of a poor young woman under the age of twenty-two having a baby out of wedlock go up by 12 percent. This included both Caucasian and African American mothers[20]

Mary Eberstadt, Senior Fellow at the Faith and Reason Institute concurs, writing, "It...doesn't take a Ph.D. to grasp that the fractured family is a major engine of the increased welfare state. Why? Because overall, the state is the financial backer that makes single motherhood—and absent fatherhood—possible."[21] She continues that the state assumes a role of a "flush, but controlling super-daddy" by bankrolling single parenting, and thereby perpetuating it.

She concludes, "Economists are fond of saying if we want more of something, we should subsidize it. And, though it's been done with the best intentions that is exactly what the welfare state has been doing across the free societies of the West: subsidizing family breakdown."[22]

Even liberal Chicago Mayor Rahm Emanuel understands the impact of family breakdown and resulting societal chaos. After a particularly bloody weekend when seventy people were shot, he addressed the out-of-control violence in the city that has reached epidemic proportions by stating the problem was ultimately a moral one. He said:

> This may not be politically correct, but I know the power of
> what faith and family can do.... Our kids need that struc-
> ture...I am asking...that we don't shy away from a full
> discussion about the importance of faith and family to
> develop and nurture character, self-respect, a value system,
> and a moral compass that allows kids to know good from
> bad and right from wrong.[23]

It has been well documented how the rise of fatherless homes has
led to a concurrent rise in incarceration rates for African American
males. Cynthia Harper of the University of Pennsylvania and Sara S.
McLanahan of Princeton University found that young men who grow
up in fatherless homes are twice as likely to end up in jail as those who
come from traditional two-parent families.[24] Numerous other studies
back up this assertion.

These problems are not isolated to the African American community; it is simply that for African Americans the problem is most
acute. Out-of-wedlock births are now rampant among all racial groups.
In 2014, 65.7 percent of babies born to women under the age of twenty-
five and 36.7 percent of babies born to women between the ages of
twenty-five and twenty-nine were outside of marriage. Overall, 40.2
percent of all children were born out of wedlock.[25] The Centers for
Disease Control found 25 percent of all American babies since 2010
were born to cohabiting couples—the highest rate ever, more than
double the rate from just ten years earlier.[26] And, according to the U.S.
Census Bureau, the poverty rate for children living with two unmarried, cohabiting parents is similar to the rate of those living in a
single-parent home.[27]

However, when politicians, activists, and social commentators talk
about inequality, they often leave out the critical role married parents
play in keeping children above the poverty line. There is evidence the

breakdown of the nuclear family in American society is, in fact, the primary reason why the gulf between the "haves" and "have-nots" has widened over the past fifty years. Robert Rector of the Heritage Foundation has written about how the breakdown in marriage and the rise of out-of-wedlock births has resulted in a society of castes. According to Rector, in the top half of society, married, college-educated couples raise children. Contrastingly, in the bottom half are children raised by single mothers with a high school degree or less.[28]

But before we continue, we want to stop for a moment and state there are single mothers who have done an incredible and heroic job of raising their children. They have been successful, regardless of how difficult the circumstances, and by no means are we critical of those who are doing the best they can—often in situations where they are single parents by circumstance, and not by choice.

We have known a single mother who raised a young man who eventually became an Army Ranger and decorated war hero who sadly lost his life fighting for our country, and another who raised a fine young man who presently pitches for the New York Yankees. There are countless other stories of heroic single mothers who worked three jobs just to make ends meet, but still had time to invest in and instill solid values in their children. And as a result, their children succeeded in life. These single mothers are an inspiration to us all and are true heroes.

Nevertheless, Dr. Peter H. Schuck, professor emeritus at Yale Law School, writes in his book *One Nation Undecided: Clear Thinking about Five Hard Issues That Divide Us* that "the family is the essential core of any society, and the steady decline of two-parent households is probably the single most consequential social trend of the half-century." He goes on to show evidence that regardless of race, children with no father present in the home are almost five times more likely to be poor than the children of married couples. In addition, the children of female-headed households account for well over half of all children in poverty. He concludes, "Indeed, the single best predictor of low upward mobility in a given geographic area is a faction of children with a single parent." [29]

The issue of missing fathers has serious consequences for society. Single mothers can be great mothers, but in a single-parent household there is something lacking—something necessary for children's emotional and mental development. Fatherless girls often become severely depressed, self-destructive, and sexually promiscuous as they seek to fill the void left by the absence of loving father. [30] Boys, on the other hand, tend to deal with that void through anger and rage. Many of the tragic shootings or horrible abuses of women we have seen over the past several years have been instigated by boys from broken homes. [31]

In 2017, a study done by the American Enterprise Institute took a penetrating look into four areas of American life: families, community, employment, and faith. The report used data to illustrate the upward trajectory of out-of-wedlock births and the downward trajectory of marriages. While we have already discussed the alarming rise in out-of-wedlock births, equally troubling is the increase in cohabitation and the decline in marriages.

In 1970, there were nearly seventy-seven marriages for every one thousand women fifteen years of age or older. As of 2015, that number has decreased to thirty-two marriages per one thousand—the lowest rate in American history. [32]

The decreasing marriage rate has also led to a spike in the percentage of people living alone. According to the 2013 U.S. Census Population Survey, 27 percent of all Americans now live alone, compared with just 5 percent in the 1920s. [33] While not all adults living alone are lonely, many are, and individuals living alone are much more likely to lack significant social connections, which can be deadly. John Cacioppo, a University of Chicago professor, wrote in his book *Loneliness* that the negative health risks of living alone are far worse than air pollution or obesity.[34]

While it is difficult to measure in research studies the impact of moral relativism and cultural secularism on the breakdown of marriage and the family, both have played a significant role. The Sexual Revolution of the 1960s and 1970s exacerbated the trends Moynihan saw in the African American community that have now transcended all races. As Moynihan feared, family disintegration has led to social regression—much of which we have already discussed—in our inner cities and rural communities. While this social regression affects all ages and races, its most tragic victims are the ones least capable of dealing with its ramifications: the children of America's lower economic classes, who must live with the fallout from acute poverty and rampant drug addiction.

The *New York Times* reported that between 2004 and 2013, the number of babies born with drug dependencies because their mothers were addicted rose nearly seven-fold in rural counties and four-fold in urban areas.[35] The main cause is the opioid crisis, which has cut a deadly swath through the small communities making up rural America. In 2016, according to the Centers for Disease Control, there were more than sixty-three thousand deaths from opioids in the United States.[36] In 2000, there were fewer than five thousand deaths from opioids.[37]

According to the *Times* article, fifteen out of every one hundred babies in poorer areas, such as the Appalachians, are born addicted to opioids.[38] Perhaps not coincidentally, Kentucky and West Virginia, two states where the opioid crisis is at its most acute, have seen marriage rates decline by more than 25 percent over the last four decades.[39] While economic misfortune and the loss of blue collar jobs are contributing factors, there seems to be a direct line connecting the decline of marriage to the despair that results in increased drug use.

Children born with a dependence on drugs face tremendous hardship from the beginning, starting just minutes after birth. As soon as the umbilical cord is cut, these newborns must go through withdrawal, an experience described by adult former addicts as "living in hell." [40] Babies can experience vomiting, tremors, and violent temperature changes. After their traumatic first days of life, these children may experience higher rates of emotional disturbance, anxiety, depression, learning disabilities, and development challenges. [41]

Combined, these factors result in these children having developmental issues affecting all aspects of their lives while contributing to them becoming drug users themselves later in life. [42]

Thus, the breakdown of marriage and family and the resulting social regression lead to what Rector described as a caste society. Numerous studies have shown that children in single-parent homes are more likely to engage in substance abuse than those in stable, two-parent (mother and father) homes. [43] These children eventually grow up into adults and bring their drug dependency with them, creating another generation of children trapped in the cycle of family dysfunction and drug abuse. It is a triple whammy resulting in a continued downward spiral of despair and loss of social capital with each succeeding generation.

The result is a chasm between those who are born healthy and are nurtured in a two-parent home, and those who emerge from the womb with three strikes already against them: drug-addicted, trapped in poverty, and lacking an essential parent. And the cycle only gets worse as time goes on.

Thus, a society is formed where the dividing line between the haves and have-nots is determined at the very beginning of life. If children are born into a stable, two-parent family, they are likely to be successful in life. If they are born into the instability of a continued cycle of a broken family, they will likely fall prey to the resulting pathologies.

All this information is overwhelming, and we have only been able to present snippets of the problems plaguing marriages, families, and society as a whole in this chapter. Nevertheless, it is evident family cohesion or disintegration is now the definitive barometer of the health or illness of the social fabric of our country, and this disintegration is not ideological, but societal.

As Timothy Carney writes:

> When it comes to putting "family values" into practice, the divide is not along ideological lines. Liberal elites are practicing what the Religious Right has long preached: Finish school, get a job, get married, have kids, and stay involved in the kids' lives. Conservative elites and many communities of religious conservatives live this family-centric model with traditional timing of schooling, marriage, and children.

He adds, "We are left, then, with a society where intact families are not the norm but are something of a luxury good. That's hardly a healthy foundation."[44]

But there is another factor to consider: the decline in church attendance and the influence of faith in society over the past half century. Carney writes that as the family disintegrates, the last line of defense is our nation's churches as the only major institutions providing support to keeping families intact—which is the essential building block of society.

Research bears this fact out. A Harvard School of Public Health study found couples who regularly attend church services are about 30–50 percent less likely to divorce.[45] This statistic holds true across racial groups. He also cites research done by Professors Kenneth Pargament and Annette Mahoney of Bowling Green University's Spirituality and Psychology Research Team that marriages are stronger and happier when husbands and wives understand that there is a deeper spiritual significance to marriage beyond feelings or economic security.[46]

Why do faith and church attendance play such a critical role? The Harvard study surmises it's because religious teachings are sacred, an important bond is created in the marriage vows, and attending religious services reinforces that bond. Religious teachings across all faiths discourage divorce and have strong teachings against adultery. They also provide family support through connections with other families and, perhaps most important, place a strong emphasis on love and putting the needs of others above one's own.[47]

Our friend and colleague Glenn Stanton, director of Global Family Formation Studies at Focus on the Family, concludes, "Faith *does* matter.... It's one of the most powerful secret weapons in marital happiness and longevity—and this should no longer be a secret to anyone." [48]

Unfortunately, over the past several decades, the understanding of marriage as a sacred bond between a man and a woman has been lost as it has become more about personal happiness and "fulfillment." As James Q. Wilson put it, "Marriage was once a sacrament, then it became a contract, and now it is an arrangement. Once religion provided the sacrament, then the law enforced the contract, and now personal preferences define the arrangement." He concludes:

> The right and best way for a culture to restore itself is for it to be rebuilt, not from the top down by government policies, but from the bottom up by personal decisions. On the side of that effort, we can find churches—or at least many of them—and the common experience of adults that the essence of marriage is not sex, or money, or even children: it is commitment.[49]

The renewal of faith is the essential part of solving the breakdown of marriage and the family. Despite the fact that faith and churches can play such a critical role in keeping marriages and families intact, church attendance continues to decline. The American Enterprise Institute Report, mentioned earlier, found that forty years ago 70 percent of adults were members of churches or temples and more than half of them attended services at the very least monthly.[50] Currently, just over half of Americans belong to a church or synagogue, and monthly attendance has fallen by more than 20 percent since just before World War II.[51]

To restore marriage and the family and begin to reverse the tragic trends of the past fifty-plus years, our efforts must start here with the renewal of the family and a restoration of religious faith. By solving this problem, we can then restore social capital and effectively address issues such as inner-city crime, drug addiction, income inequality, and incivility.

For Christians, the effort to restore marriage, family, and social capital must start in our own lives. If we cannot model God's plan for marriage and the raising and nurturing of children, then we have nothing to offer to those trapped in poverty, addiction, and broken homes. If we are not involved in a church, we miss out on not only the biblical teaching needed to keep us focused on God instead of self, but also the opportunity to develop mutually encouraging relationships with other couples. Finally, church attendance and practicing our faith in our home is a critical component of future success for our children in their relationships.

Practicing our faith in our homes is key. It has often been said— and it has been proven to be true—that values are "caught, not taught." As well-known Christian author and speaker Josh McDowell has said, "Rules without relationship leads to rebellion."[52] It is essential we as parents model our faith to our children through words and actions.

This means we must have relationships with our children, which takes time and requires putting our personal agendas aside and putting their needs above our own. If we only offer rules without love or without reasoning behind them, our children will not see how those guidelines can help them make good decisions in life—decisions which lead to future success for not only them, but for their children, as well. Along the way, as we model the biblical truths of marriage and family, even those around us who have no connections to the faith community will see and be influenced. Co-workers, folks in our neighborhoods, childhood friends, those we engage in retail and service businesses, and so forth, are watching whether we know it or not. Truth has a way of attracting attention.

Those of us in strong and stable marriages need to come alongside younger couples who are just starting out and offer encouragement and support. We also need to come alongside single parents, who are facing herculean tasks, and be willing to step up however necessary to support them and their children.

Finally, for those who are ready to face the challenge, there are literally thousands of children in our nation's foster care system desperately waiting to find a loving home.

In the prologue, we mentioned the couple who adopted six children—all born in difficult circumstances and of different races—and has now successfully raised them into adulthood. They faced numerous challenges and the road was often hard, but their unconditional love has made a difference in six lives that likely would have known nothing but despair. Imagine how many more lives can be changed through such self-sacrifice. There are numerous ministries, including Focus on the Family,[53] Project 1.27,[54] Bethany Christian Services,[55] and many others that help with uniting foster care children with loving Christian homes.

Any hope for the restoration of marriage, the family, and for our social capital will likely come from families with active, involved dads;

churches that foster family cohesiveness; families that live out and model their faith; and ministries that come alongside to offer guidance and wisdom to help families successfully navigate the challenges of life.

This must be accompanied by a renewed appreciation for parenting, a commitment to hard work and excellence in school, a strong work ethic and sense of personal responsibility for one's actions, and respect not just of authority, but for our fellow human beings. These are the virtues that are key not only to economic mobility and to stability, but for social advancement, as well.

While it may take a long time to reverse the damage done to marriages, families, and our social capital, change can happen one life at a time, and we, as people of faith, can be the ones who initiate that change—something no government program can accomplish—no matter the cost.

CHAPTER SIX

Restoring the Concept of the Gentleman

"All good things which are connected with manners and civilization have…depended upon…the spirit of the gentleman, and the spirit of religion." [1]
—**Edmund Burke**

"It is almost a definition of a gentleman to say he is one who never inflicts pain." [2]
—**Cardinal John Henry Newman**

"A society does not run into real trouble…until its culture begins to adopt the unmarried male pattern, until the long-term commitments on which any enduring community is based are undermined by an opportunistic public philosophy. The public philosophy of an unmarried male focuses on immediate gratification: 'What did posterity ever do for me?' A society that widely adopts this attitude is in trouble." [3]
—**George Gilder**

Edmund Burke, the great British parliamentarian and philosopher, once said the greatest cultural achievements of Western civilization were the advancement of Christianity and the concept of the gentleman.[4] He saw the two as intimately related. What Burke meant by the latter was not the stereotypical prim, proper, and emotionally distant Englishman attired in tails and a top hat, but rather something essential to the nature of humanity.

Burke believed a true gentleman made the best citizen because he made countless excellent contributions to his family, church, community, and country through self-sacrifice, personal discipline, and internal strength while exhibiting a tender heart. But Burke also knew gentlemen are not born—they are made. And he also knew faith played a major role in transforming boys into men—and ultimately *gentlemen*.

It has also been said a gentleman is a man who is strong, under control, and under the authority of his Master, Jesus Christ, who provided the perfect example of what it takes to be not only a man, but a gentleman in the truest sense of the word.

While not every man has been or is a gentleman, the concept was an ideal for men to try to emulate. Unfortunately, over the past several decades, that concept has fallen into disfavor. The result is men who have no idea what it takes to be a gentleman.

Much has been written about the "crisis" of boys and young men. We see that crisis played out throughout our culture as we have witnessed many boys and young men "fail to launch" into adulthood, seem directionless and unwilling to accept personal responsibility, engage in violent acts, and fall into increasing despair. These issues end up causing all sorts of societal issues such as fatherless children, substance abuse, and ever-increasing incarceration rates.

But these are just symptoms and are not the root cause of the problem. To cure the problem, we must regain an understanding of the concept of a gentleman. And as discussed in the previous chapter, the discussion starts with broken marriages and families.

Much of the lack of gentlemen can be attributed to young men lacking male role models to guide them and point them in the right direction. Because of the breakdown of the family, this problem now encompasses two generations because many men in their thirties and forties did not have these role models, and as a result have no idea how to be a role model to their boys.

Thus, these boys grow up in a world that values accomplishments over personal character, career over family, and autonomy over responsibility. What is communicated to them is the antithesis of being a gentleman—a man who respects women, loves children, and takes his role as a provider and nurturer of his family seriously.

Instead of *"How much money will I make?"* or *"How fast can I climb the corporate ladder?"* or *"How can I find self-fulfillment?"* the questions young men should be asking themselves are of the spiritual and moral ilk: *"How do I become a good man?" "How can I make a lifelong contribution to my family and society?"* and *"What is my ultimate purpose in life?"* These are the questions Tim has pondered and tried to instill in his sons as he sees them grow into young men.

These last questions are vitally important. When young men find their purpose in life, they become disciplined and focused. They realize their lives are not their own. They come to model self-sacrifice and unconditional love to those around them. They become what is called a "good citizen." They become a *gentleman.*

When these questions are not asked and these behaviors are not modeled to young boys and men by others, young men often enter adulthood with little or no purpose. Instead of being strong, in control, and under the authority of their Master, these men are weak in spirit, prone to temptation, out of control in their actions, and bow to no authority but their own. And the results are tragic for men, but in all too many cases for women, as well.

This was seen in the last days of 2017 when it seemed every newscast, newspaper, magazine, or website was blasting news about another horrific incident of powerful men sexually exploiting and abusing women.

There is no denying there have always been corrupt men who viewed the world—and particularly women—as objects to be exploited for personal pleasure. This is, simply put, evil. No man who takes such a view of the world and of his fellow human beings can ever consider himself a gentleman. One of the most tragic misinterpretations of the term "gentleman" is so-called "gentlemen's clubs," which are not the venues for gentlemen.

What these stories tragically reminded us was that while there may be plenty of biological men around, there are far too few gentlemen in America today.

At the same time, there are true gentlemen who see the inherent worth and dignity—*imago Dei*—in every person, man or woman. These men strive to treat everyone with the utmost respect, personally and professionally, and seek to create the conditions for human flourishing for everyone with whom they interact. They do so because of the values passed down to them from generation to generation from other gentlemen.

Peggy Noonan echoed these sentiments, but added a few more of her own, in her definition of a gentleman. She wrote, "A gentleman is good to women because he has his own dignity and sees theirs."[5] She adds, "[A gentleman] takes opportunities to show [women] respect. He is not pushy, manipulative, or belittling. He stands with them not because they are weak, but because they deserve friendship."[6]

Noonan goes on to share a story of a male columnist who gave her helpful critiques of her work and, in her words, "urged her on." In her view, "a gentleman is an encourager of women."[7]

Unfortunately, over the past several decades, our society has energized bad behavior through such evils as pornography, graphic sexuality and violence in popular entertainment, and allowing men to find ways to abdicate personal responsibility for their actions—particularly in the area of sexuality. Meanwhile, the good values that transform a man into a gentleman are mocked—and, in some instances, vilified—as being disrespectful toward women. They are anything but.

In the days after the horrific sexual abuse stories mentioned earlier became known, some individuals started to take a deeper look at how our society empowers bad behavior.

Writing for *National Review*, conservative Jewish commentator Ben Shapiro cited how the rules considered standard for centuries for governing behavior—and in particular, male behavior and the relationship between the sexes—have been lost. The loss of these rules for good behavior has enabled the bad behavior of men to flourish.

According to Shapiro, those carefully cultivated rules of conduct between the sexes included the expectation that men would be chivalrous protectors of women, men and women interacted within parameters designed to protect women, and sex was reserved until marriage.

Of this last rule, Shapiro explains it is more than simply an old-fashioned moral expectation; that rule strengthens and serves society by cementing the connection between sex and commitment. In addition, it provides objective evidence before a community of witnesses that a woman has given positive consent to sexual activity, clearing up much of the haziness surrounding the idea of "consent" today.[8]

During the Sexual Revolution, all these rules were tossed aside. Instead of seeing them as social parameters encouraging respect for women and providing a measure of protection, the rules were perceived as patriarchal, demeaning of women, and in Shapiro's words, "artificial barriers to progress."[9] In the new order of things, men and women would be treated exactly the same way—a promise that, as we have seen, has rebounded badly for both sexes.

While the old rules provided mutual consent and security, the new rules say marriage allows men to throw all caution to the wind. Therefore, the institution of marriage—which governed proper behavior between the sexes since the beginning of time—must be denigrated and ultimately discarded. In addition, sexual taboos were oppressive and chivalry perpetuated the stereotype that women are weak and powerless—when, instead, chivalry was a way for a man to express how highly he valued the dignity and worth of a woman.

The result of these new rules is that society as a whole no longer upholds a code of behavior for men that expects them to maintain self-control or to be encouragers and protectors of women. Society now says "anything goes" with regard to sexual desires and people should be able to have sex as they please with no commitment required—the only requirement is the "consent" of the other party.

This amorphous standard of "consent" has turned out to be disastrously unclear, with the potential utterly to destroy a man's life if a woman decides after the fact that she did not consent to the sexual encounter—even if she gave every indication of consent in the moment. By tying sexual behavior only to consent—and not to the commitment of the marital bond—the mutual respect between the sexes breaks down into chaos.

Far from freeing us from rigid, stultifying moral expectations for sexual behavior, the rejection of the social expectation that sex occurs only within marriage (understood as the life-long union between one man and one woman) has resulted in a mire of emotional and physical devastation.

As Shapiro writes, "Tearing down fences only lets those sins break out of their confines…as we're finding out, are the wages of destroying boundaries on human behavior not freedom, but anarchy—and, for too many women, oppression by voracious men?" [10]

In the mid-twentieth century, C. S. Lewis predicted the outcome of the trend toward separating sex from marriage. He wrote in *The Abolition of Man*, "In a sort of ghastly simplicity, we remove the organ and demand the function. We make men without chests and expect of them virtue and enterprise. We laugh at honor and are shocked to find traitors in our midst. We castrate and bid the geldings to be fruitful." [11] This statement, while written decades ago, supremely sums up the state of men in early twenty-first century America caught up in the devastating wake of the Sexual Revolution.

Treating women with respect, dignity, and tenderness is a result of the honor code of a gentleman. It is also the model provided by Jesus. His treatment of women serves as the highest and best expression and model of what it means truly to be a gentleman in his interactions with women. He not only formed friendships with women, He saw them as "*imago Dei*"—with inherent dignity and worth. There are numerous examples of this throughout the Gospels, including the raising of the widow's son (Luke 7:11-15), His anointing by the prostitute (Luke 7:36-50), and the death and resurrection of Lazarus (John 11).

But the disappearance of consistent, morally coherent expectations for proper behavior is just one cause of the paucity of gentlemen in our society. Another contributing factor is the lack of mentors for young boys.

For most of American history, husbands, fathers, grandfathers, uncles, coaches, pastors, teachers, and mentors understood the virtues they were expected to embody in their own person and to instill in the young men around them.

Ideally, the first and best mentor, of course, is a father. The former commissioner of baseball Fay Vincent shared that his late father admonished him to "always be a gentleman."[12] Generations of American men heard the same message from their own dads. They knew being a gentleman meant decency, excellence in their work, and valuing and preserving the family name. It was about integrity over intellect and embodying goodwill in both the highest of highs and lowest of lows in life.

Unfortunately, many boys today—even those from intact homes—do not have a father or another man in their lives who can guide them through the critical developmental steps that transform them into gentlemen. That is because these men, as mentioned earlier, did not have fathers who—either for emotional or physical reasons (divorce, born out of wedlock are two examples)—could serve as mentors. In these situations, it becomes necessary for other men to step into the gap.

Craig's grandfather died when Craig's father was twelve years old, at the most critical stage of a boy's development. In addition, it was during the depths of the Great Depression. Craig's father did not have someone who could mentor him through the stormy seas of adolescence—a particularly challenging adolescence as he, the oldest son, shouldered a great burden of responsibility and went to work to support his mother, sister, and infant brother.

Though he learned to manage the challenges of life and ended up being a P-38 pilot in World War II, the loss of his father at a young age left deep scars. Craig's dad was abusive, angry, and had no idea how to model being a gentleman since there was no one to guide him during his formative years.

But Craig had a dear and godly granduncle, his Uncle Chris, who modeled to him what it meant to be a man who loved his wife, guided his children, had good humor, and was a person who always put others before himself. He filled the void Craig's father could not. That was supplemented by Craig's faith in Christ, who completed the modeling for him. To this day, while Craig loves his father (who passed away in 1998) and especially respects his work ethic and his service to our country in World War II, he credits his granduncle with being the mentor he needed to become a gentleman.

Tim, on the other hand, was blessed to have a father who was a gentleman role model. Because of that modeling, Tim has been able to pass that heritage down to his sons, as well.

We all can play a role in helping to train boys to be gentlemen. We can do so as a father, an uncle or granduncle, a teacher, or simply a neighbor who models to young boys the traits that will make them confident, morally upright, and capable of encouraging—rather than abusing or ignoring—women. We can teach them to be firm but fair and compassionate fathers to their own children and help them become respected members of the community.

Great gentlemen make great citizens. And great citizens bring about cultural transformation—starting first in their homes, then permeating all aspects of society. We need a generation of gentlemen who will welcome responsibility and seeks to perform with seriousness, earnestness, excellence, piety, patriotism, courage, duty, self-sacrifice, and faith in God.

Let us strive to be the people who provide the necessary guidance to turn boys not just into men, but into gentlemen. If we succeed, it will wheel us away from decline and despair and toward the kind of recovery and renaissance that will bring about restoration in other areas of American society, as well.

CHAPTER SEVEN

Restoring Virtue

"But what is liberty without wisdom, and without virtue? It is the greatest of all possible evils; for it is folly, vice, and madness, without tuition or restraint." [1]
—**Edmund Burke**

"Liberty can no more exist without virtue than the body can live and move without a soul." [2]
—**John Adams**

The loss of respect for religious freedom, life, and the boundaries for human sexuality are all symptoms of the loss of virtue. For restoration to occur, we must regain an understanding and appreciation of a virtuous society.

In a surprising twist, after decades of downplaying or even degrading the role of virtue in a stable and healthy society, a number of voices from within the mainstream media have reverted to using virtue-based language. They have come to this realization as the loss of virtue can be seen throughout our nation—whether it be the lack of civility toward others, the lack of respect and disregard for boundaries between the sexes, or the increasing disregard for human life. Christine Emba, a columnist for the *Washington Post*—hardly a faith-based publication—wrote in November 2018, "Now could be the time to reintroduce virtues such as prudence, temperance, respect, and even love." [3]

Well-known syndicated columnist Cal Thomas added in another column:

> In the train wreck of our present culture, we are witnessing the failure over the last 50 years to instruct and discipline our children in ways that as adults they are more likely to embrace the values that can lead to a virtuous life. Why did we expect any other outcome after mostly abandoning those virtues? If you penalize and discourage virtuous things you will get less virtue; conversely, if you subsidize and encourage virtue, you will get more of it.[4]

This sentiment, expressed by a columnist in the mainstream American media, contains surprising echoes of C. S. Lewis's words mentioned in the last chapter from *The Abolition of Man*, where he laments the presence of "men without chests" in society.[5] What Lewis was referring to was that without a belief in and the teaching of universal moral laws, we fail to educate the heart and are left with intelligent men who behave like animals, i.e. "men without chests."

While it is nice to read appeals to classical virtue ethics, there is one reality that lies at the heart of all virtue ethics systems: virtue cannot be the basis of ethics within a relativistic culture. When everyone is left to their own self-determination of what virtue and ethics are, you end up with no virtues at all and all sorts of atrocities can be justified. A manifestation of this was a group of philosophy students at Hamilton College who were reluctant to judge Hitler for murdering six million Jews. "Of course I dislike the Nazis," one student observed, "but who is to say they are morally wrong?"[6]

There must a transcendent, unchanging, and objective source for those virtues or these systems will rapidly degenerate to the utilitarian ethical system we live in today where whatever is useful for providing pleasure or perceived value is ethical. The source for the virtue system on which America was built and to which we must return if we hope to restore our culture is God.

A broad survey of America's Founders—regardless of their own personal faith and imperfections—shows they understood that faith in God was the foundation for a virtuous society. They appealed to God as a transcendent source of virtue and universal values throughout our nation's founding documents. This was done most famously in the Declaration of Independence, which includes the well-known words, "We hold these Truths to be self-evident, that all men are created equal, that they are endowed by their Creator with certain unalienable rights, that among these are life, liberty, and the pursuit of happiness."

While not all the Founders were virtuous in their behavior, most of them understood the vital role virtue plays in creating and maintaining an ordered society. Signer Benjamin Franklin, whose personal life was not always notably virtuous and whose personal creed is difficult to pin down, nevertheless understood the importance of virtue within a society. He wrote, "Only a virtuous people are capable of freedom." [7] Franklin recognized there is a continuous line from the practice of virtue to a society that allows freedom to flourish. Without virtue, man cannot exercise his unalienable rights of life, liberty, and the pursuit of happiness.

So, what is virtue? Saint Thomas Aquinas defined moral virtues as "settled dispositions (good habits) of various appetitive powers which incline and allow their possessors to make good moral choices." [8] Virtuous people are those who have learned to put the needs of others above their own while moderating their behavior in a manner that keeps them from making poor moral choices that would not only negatively impact them, but would impact society, as a whole.

A virtuous society is one in which individuals learn to value personal duty and selflessness. People think about the world in terms of how they, flourishing as individuals, can enhance and support others. Today, however, our society promotes a relentless "all about me" philosophy that celebrates self-indulgence, personal ambition, and self-fulfillment as the ultimate end of human existence. This has led to a diminished appreciation for institutions like marriage and parenthood—both of which require self-sacrifice—and for faith systems that encourage people to adhere to moral standards that may limit or restrict the "free expression" of their appetites.

What are the virtues that for centuries upheld Western societies? While not everyone uses the same terms, traditionally the four cardinal virtues—taken from Plato's *Republic* and Saint Augustine—are prudence, justice, fortitude, and temperance. While they placed them in different order, they agreed on what the four cardinal virtues were.

These four virtues, though not explicitly based in Christian theology, have long been understood as being complementary to the fruits of the Spirit listed by the Apostle Paul in Galatians 5:22–23: "But the fruit of the Spirit is love, joy, peace, patience, kindness, goodness, faithfulness, gentleness, self-control" (ESV). In addition, the cardinal virtues work in unison with the theological virtues of faith, hope, and charity (love).

Scripture is clear that virtues go hand in hand with creedal convictions in the life of the Christian. In 2 Peter 1:4–8, the Apostle Peter says:

> For this very reason, make every effort to supplement your faith with virtue, and virtue with knowledge, and knowledge with self-control, and self-control with steadfastness, and steadfastness with godliness, and godliness with brotherly affection, and brotherly affection with love. For if these qualities are yours and are increasing, they keep you from being ineffective or unfruitful in the knowledge of our Lord Jesus Christ (ESV).

Historically, the Christian church has a robust tradition of integrating the cardinal virtues into this scriptural view of holiness and the human person. Those four virtues—prudence, courage, temperance, and justice—correspond neatly with Christian ideals of human behavior as modeled by Christ and admonished by Scripture. So it is worth studying each of them, both individually and in relation to each other, as we consider what must be present at the core of a virtuous society.

The Greek philosopher Aristotle defined prudence as "the right reason applied to practice." [9] Prudence was also identified by Plato and Cicero as the first cardinal virtue. Later on, Saint Thomas Aquinas placed prudence as the first cardinal virtue because it is concerned with cognition and intellect. It is the virtue that allows individuals to judge and distinguish between right and wrong in situations they encounter daily.

Prudence requires individuals to seek the counsel of others, as it is impossible for any one person to have perfect knowledge of every possible moral situation. In contemporary language, prudence is the reason for the value people place on having accountability partners who encourage us to think clearly about morality. Such accountability lessens the potential we will fall into sin or error because it helps us look outside of our selfish desires.

In many ways, prudence is the opposite of pride. In a virtuous society, before making decisions, people consult with those who are known to be sound, reliable judges of what is moral and what is not. Everyone who wishes to grow in the virtue of prudence must have these people in their lives. Prudent advisors are individuals who push us to consider the reality of a moral situation more fully; they cannot be people who simply go along with our inclinations and affirm what we already think is true. Part of growing in the virtue of prudence is having the humility to listen to what these individuals have to say—even if it hurts or disappoints us.

Conversely, pride is the epitome of imprudence because the imprudent person cannot bear to hear that he or she may be wrong in desire, thought, or deed. A habit of dismissing counsel simply because it does not affirm what we want to do is a sign of imprudence, which often leads to poorly considered and even vicious decisions. Imprudence, or the inability to perceive and adhere to the good in decision-making, leads us—both as individuals and as a society—to try to justify all sorts of vicious behavior, such as adultery, ethical lapses, anger, and racism, to name just a few.

To illustrate what imprudence looks like in action, we have only to consider the all-too-common situation of a religious leader committing a grievous sin and even embracing a lifestyle of that sin. In many of these situations, these prominent leaders have acted imprudently by having no accountability structures in place. They are often prideful and have surrounded themselves with people who say what they want to hear, rather than with people who will challenge them to think about moral situations differently.

A prudent person is one who is humble, listens to counsel, and then acts accordingly. But prudence is not only active before a decision is made; it affects how a person lives with his decision afterward. If a prudent person realizes he has made a mistake, he accepts responsibility for his actions—including the resulting negative consequences—without complaint. An imprudent person believes he is right in all matters, rejects the counsel of others, and then does whatever he feels is best or "right in his own eyes." When things go wrong, he tends to blame others rather than accept responsibility for his actions.

Without prudence, we are prone to make snap decisions or say things based on our emotions of the moment, rather than after careful and deliberate thought. We become more prone to think uncritically, fall for demagoguery, or say things that can cause long-term damage to relationships. We do not rely on stable, unchanging standards of reality to evaluate what is true and what is false.

In today's world of 24/7 news, sound bites, and social media, imprudence tends to be the rule rather than the exception. Imprudence riddles our current political and cultural discourse and leads to irrational anger toward fellow citizens with whom we may disagree. Rather than engaging in reasoned discourse, we resort to blaming our fellow citizens—exacerbating problems rather than solving them. There is perhaps no more urgent time in American history for citizens and leaders to seek the restoration of prudence as a societal virtue.

The next of the cardinal virtues is justice. Aristotle defined justice as a "moral disposition which renders men apt to do just things and which causes them to act justly and to wish what is just." [10]

The concept of *imago Dei* is a component of the Christian conception of justice, for it is what makes it possible for us to view each individual as having inherent dignity and unalienable rights. If we are all, in fact, created in God's image, what we believe or think about another person should not affect whether we treat them justly. Father John Hardon, who described justice as the "constant and permanent determination to give everyone his or her rightful due," perhaps best summarizes this concept. [11]

Justice can only be present in an unselfish action. Unfortunately, throughout human history and particularly in recent years, it has been twisted by some to be just the opposite. This plays itself out in our culture through constant demands that governments and other institutions must address whatever injustice an individual feels they have received, and, in turn, punish those who they perceive to have perpetuated said "injustice." But the virtue of justice is not meant to be for us—it is meant to be for others.

In practical terms, we should seek to do just things. Thus, it is justice that inspires us to stand up for those who cannot speak for themselves, such as the innocent child in a woman's womb who faces the loss of its unalienable right to life. It was justice that inspired millions of Americans to take a stand for civil rights in the 1950s and 1960s and for people like Billy Graham to remove the ropes that separated whites from blacks at his crusades. Justice means standing up for the rights of conscience of those compelled by force to violate their unalienable right to religious liberty. It means standing up for those facing persecution for their beliefs. That is the virtue of justice in action.

The third cardinal virtue is fortitude. Fortitude is the strength to choose the good even in the face of difficulty and danger. It allows us to overcome our fears and remain steadfast in our principles despite the obstacles we face. It works in unity with prudence and justice by giving us the strength to do what we have perceived is right.

The virtue of fortitude is active in our lives whenever we face a situation where it is easier to do the wrong thing than to stand strong for what we believe and do the right thing anyway. Fortitude enables us to pursue the good, the true, and the beautiful during those times.

Fortitude can be imagined as the backbone of the other cardinal virtues supporting and holding each of them upright against the gravity of challenges and opposition. It holds up justice, for example, when a person stands up against racial injustice because they know all individuals are created in God's image. It supports prudence when a person goes against his or her own inclinations to follow the wisdom and advice of a respected accountability partner.

It enables a young woman who is facing an unplanned pregnancy to ignore advice to abort her child and choose life, despite the difficulties and complications this will introduce into her life. It gives a creative professional the strength to adhere to her deeply held beliefs when asked to go against those beliefs by communicating support for something she does not believe is right.

Christ modeled fortitude for us through his willingness to stand up boldly to the Pharisees and other leaders of his time and proclaim God's Truth. He modeled fortitude when he stood up to Satan and his temptations during his forty days in the desert.

The fourth cardinal virtue is temperance. This virtue is what permits us to moderate our behavior, allowing us to find the proper balance in life by not over-indulging in good things or participating in bad things. While fortitude restrains our fears and provides us with moral and spiritual strength to act boldly, courageously, and rightly, temperance places a natural restraint on our desires and passions. Temperance enables us to keep our emotions in check, to speak carefully, and to withstand the desires of the flesh.

Therefore, temperance is a stabilizing influence. It is temperance that keeps us from responding with anger when we are wronged or feel attacked. It is temperance that gives us the self-discipline to avoid those things tempting us to sin. It is temperance that allows us to remain focused on the needs of others rather than on our self-perceived needs.

It is clear by now how these four virtues, though not explicitly Christian, fit into a Christian vision of holiness. When all four virtues are working in unison through God's grace, they make it possible for us to adhere to scriptural standards such as being slow to anger, acting unselfishly, standing boldly on conviction, and keeping our desires under control.

For example, a virtuous husband and father puts the emotional and physical needs of his wife and children above his own. A virtuous member of a community treats all people the same, regardless of their position in life, and stands against injustice. A virtuous citizen chooses to stand for what is right—no matter the personal cost—rather than compromise for the sake of personal comfort. A virtuous individual practices restraint, being slow to anger, guarding his tongue, and avoiding those areas that may lead him to destructive behavior.

Ultimately, we cannot have a virtuous society without first return-ing as people of faith to the practice of these virtues in our own lives. If we do not embody these qualities, if we do not model these virtues—all of which Christ modeled for us—in word and action, then we can-not expect our fellow citizens to do so either.

The road to restoring virtue starts in our own hearts not tomorrow, but today, for the time is urgent and the need is great for a virtuous America. This means as parents, we need to instill these virtues in our children at an early age so they will have a strong sense of right and wrong before they enter a world that tells them that what is right is whatever they feel at the moment. It means we must treat every indi-vidual with dignity and respect, regardless of his or her views or station in life. And it means we must exhibit self-control and personal disci-pline in all areas of our lives.

A virtuous society will be restored by a virtuous people. Let the practice of virtue in our lives be a guiding light for others to follow and ultimately embrace in their own lives. The result will be a spiritual and cultural transformation and an America that is once again a shining city on a hill.

CHAPTER EIGHT

Restoring Education

"Every education teaches a philosophy; if not by dogma then by suggestion, by implication, by atmosphere." [1]

—G. K. Chesterton

"We must recover the idea that education is about more than making a living. Education's best claim, William James said, is that it teaches a person to value what deserves to be valued." [2]

—William Bennett

One of the few areas in present American culture where much of the political Left and Right agree is that our public educational system is broken. While the sides have different solutions for solving the problems they perceive, the bottom line is there is an increasing consensus that the state of education in America is a mess.

For example, on the Left, the Center for American Progress states that while more and more jobs are requiring at least a bachelor's degree, only about one-third of American workers have one. They add that many students who have a high school diploma are not prepared for higher education, as 20 percent of first-year college students must take some sort of remedial course. They conclude, "In other words, a large percentage of students land a high school diploma that is basically meaningless. The document might indicate that the students are ready for college, but in reality, the students simply do not have the necessary skills or knowledge." [3]

On the Right, Kevin Roberts, executive director of the Texas Policy Foundation, writes that American schools as a whole are mediocre at the very best because they rank near the bottom of the developed world. American educational attainment is "stagnant, at best, and likely regressing." [4]

The failures of America's educational system have led to the loss of our nation's competitive advantage.[5] For example, literacy rates in American inner-city schools are appalling. A 2015 report by the National Center on Education Statistics found 93 percent of eighth graders are not proficient in reading.[6]

According to the 2015 Program for International Student Assessment, which tests fifteen-year-olds around the world, the math skills of American students have remained stagnant for nearly two decades, falling behind Japan, Poland, and Ireland. U.S. test scores are below the global average. The United States is twenty-fourth out of seventy-one countries in science and thirty-eighth in math. As a result, the U.S. slipped to third in the 2016-2017 Global Competitiveness Report behind Switzerland and Sweden.[7]

One symptom of our failing education system is the decreasing ability of our citizens to think critically about issues.[8] A robust education system trains students to function as morally mature individuals, giving them the intellectual tools to make sound judgments about morally complex situations and separate fact from fiction. Without these skills, often described as "critical thinking," people are inclined to follow the natural human tendency to make decisions based on their emotions and to be less able to separate fact from fiction in their perception of reality.

We see the decay of critical thinking in America in the recent phenomenon of "fake news," in which individuals spread false narratives through social media channels. "Fake news" stories succeed because they pander to the preconceived ideas of a group; when people see headlines that bolster their preconceptions, they are quick to share the stories without taking the time to determine if the claims within those stories are true—or, in some cases, even plausible.

In 2016, for example, 802,000 people on Facebook shared a story with the headline "Trump Offering Free One-Way Tickets to Africa & Mexico for Those Who Wanna Leave America." Another story with the headline "Obama Signs Executive Order Banning the Pledge of Allegiance in Schools Nationwide," posted on a fake news site that mirrors ABC News, had 2,177,000 Facebook shares, comments, and reactions from people who believed it to be true.[9]

The inability to discern truth from falsehood in media narratives is dangerously widespread. A 2017 study of millennials found only 24 percent were able to correctly answer eight of nine questions designed to gauge their ability to detect fake news. In addition, 55 percent said they relied on social media for news and 51 percent said they shared online content very or fairly often.[10]

The bottom line is regardless of where one sits on the political spectrum, America's children are paying the price as they enter adulthood. They are woefully unequipped to enter college, which is becoming increasingly essential to securing employment in an economy where low-skill jobs are quickly disappearing. When they do not secure employment, they do not become productive and responsible citizens.

In our inner cities, coupled with the breakdown of marriage and family, the state of our schools has left generations of children trapped in a cycle of poverty and despair.

To restore American education, it is important to revisit the purpose of education. While there is a great debate on the Left and Right over what that purpose is, the late George A. Panichas, professor emeritus of English at the University of Maryland and editor of *Modern Age*, provided a cogent definition, writing that education's purpose is to sustain and enhance the values of civilization.[11]

Thus, education is to teach young minds to think, read, write, reason, imagine, and argue with excellence. It is about empowering young men and women to reach their full God-given potential while also developing the character to be model citizens who contribute to society's well-being. This also means our nation's educational system must equip students to enter the workforce and become productive workers, thereby enhancing not only their abilities to succeed in life, but elevating society as a whole. Unfortunately, as previously discussed, this is not happening. While there are numerous reasons why, one reason in particular sticks out. The reason is not surprising.

An excellent starting point for discussing the current problems with our educational system might be to re-read and reconsider the findings of a powerful report which first appeared over the Fourth of July weekend more than fifty years ago. It was a groundbreaking study done by the highly regarded sociologist James Coleman and was titled "Equality of Educational Opportunity." Five decades later, its findings are more relevant than ever.

The Coleman Report was released just one year after the Moynihan Report on poverty rates among African Americans, which we discussed in the chapter on marriage, family, and social capital. Both studies challenged existing opinion and attempted to elevate the discussion out of the nitty-gritty nuances of partisan policy and reintroduce timeless questions about the central role of families, marriage, and parenting in a nation's public square and policy.

As part of the Great Society programs, which included education reform, record amounts of federal taxpayer dollars poured into the coffers of our nation's public schools. Expectations were high that with the extra federal dollars, America was on the cusp of unsurpassed academic achievement. However, the Coleman Report flew in the face of the "conventional wisdom" that the surest way to solve a problem was to throw more money at it. As we saw, that did not work for poverty. Similarly, it has not worked for education. Unfortunately, despite the Coleman Report's own clear conclusions, the Johnson administration ignored the report as it sought a larger and more expansive role for federal involvement in the nation's educational system.

Coleman and his researchers used data from over six hundred thousand students and teachers across the country. They found academic achievement was less related to the quality of a student's school and more related to the social composition of the school, the student's sense of control over his environment and future, the verbal skills of teachers, and the student's family background.

According to the report, increased spending could provide many amenities, such new buildings, increased compensation for teachers and administrators, and new labs, textbooks, and extracurricular activities—all of which *can* contribute to a thriving student body. However, these funds and the structural changes they provided could not compensate for a lack of strong families, cohesive neighborhoods, and healthy communities that make up a civil society.

Thus, Coleman's team discovered a school's success or failure was tied not to federal funding, but to the family situations of the children who attended these schools. Students from intact families did better in school; students from broken families struggled, and all the money in the federal government's coffers could not fix the problem. The report concluded that family, more than anything else, has the most direct impact on students' success—not only in school, but also in life once their school years end.[12]

Just like the Moynihan Report, the Coleman Report found strong marriages and families are the key predictors for success in life and the building of social capital, while the breakdown of these two institutions contributes to a downward spiral for all aspects of society—including education.

Coleman and his researchers were not alone in this conclusion; the following decades of sociological research confirmed his findings. Nearly forty years later, Harvard professor Robert Putnam, author of the groundbreaking sociological book *Bowling Alone,* said, if given a choice between a 10 percent increase in school budgets or a 10 percent increase in parental involvement, he would take the parental involvement.[13] Putnam's argument is buttressed by studies showing the huge difference parental involvement makes.

In his 1996 book *Beyond the Classroom: Why School Reform Has Failed and What Parents Need to Do*, Professor Laurence Steinberg of Temple University estimated, based on his research, that nearly one in three American parents have no involvement in their teenagers' lives, with a particular lack of parental involvement in teens' school lives.[14]

In 2004, Karen Bogenschneider and Carol Johnson of the University of Wisconsin–Madison conducted their own study to confirm these findings. After studying nearly eight thousand high school students in nine high schools in Wisconsin and California, Bogenschneider found with only a couple exceptions that when parents were involved in their teens' schooling, the students achieved higher grades in school.[15]

Much sociological research indicates the reality is that chaotic families, neighborhoods, and school environments cannot be remedied with larger amounts of taxpayer funding because increased funding cannot resolve the emotional and development disturbances caused by such chaos when the root cause of that chaos goes unaddressed. This is the irony of twenty-first-century progressivism, which is often *regressive,* as it advocates for more government spending as a panacea for our most important social maladies and afflictions—including our broken public educational system—while encouraging the very things causing the breakdown: sexual licentiousness and government subsidizing of single parenthood.

While there are some issues that government can provide a band-aid for through money, it cannot solve them because the cures never address the source of the problem. For instance, taxpayers spend $18 billion annually on school lunch and breakfast programs for more than thirty million young Americans.[16] While this helps solve one issue—hunger—as the government can find a way to make sure children are physically fed, it cannot solve the core issues driving the poverty that make these families unable to afford meals for their children in the first place: broken families and the resulting lack of educational achievement.

Thus, as Coleman noted, the government can build the most state-of-the-art school ever seen by mankind, but if the students arrive from their homes unequipped—and even in some instances unable to learn—the beauty of the building and scope of the amenities mean nothing.

Our education system does not merely ignore the problem of low parental involvement and its adverse effects on children's ability to learn, however. One of the unintended consequences of increased government involvement in education is such involvement actually makes it *more* difficult for parents to be involved. It exacerbates the problem, rather than alleviating it.

Writing in the *American Thinker*, Chris Talgo and Lennie Jarratt of the Heartland Institute examine how increased government oversight over education has resulted in making it more difficult, if not sometimes impossible, for parents to have any say in or be involved in their children's education. For instance, federal and state curriculum standards take away the ability for parents to have a say in what is taught locally in their children's schools. In addition, educational bureaucrats and politicians who receive massive campaign donations from teachers unions block efforts such as school choice that empower parents to make the best educational decisions for the future welfare of their children.[17]

To understand what has happened, Talgo and Jarratt look back at how public education changed radically in the twentieth century. They write, for the first century of America's history, public and private schools were run at the local level. Parents were very involved, and the government only provided minimal oversight. That changed after World War I, which is now seen as the launching point for the so-called "Progressive Era."

During that era, according to Talgo and Jarratt, education reformers such as John Dewey saw our nation's educational system as a ripe opportunity to implement their utopian (or, as Talgo and Jarratt write, "dystopian depending on your view") vision through the public education system.

Dewey and his followers saw education as a sociological tool for shaping individuals to fit into society in a certain way. In his utopian vision, which he outlined in a 1933 speech on the educational status of the four and five-year-old child to the Teachers College at Columbia University, Dewey said learning should be de-emphasized and replaced with the creation of attitudes as a way of creating social change.[18]

In order to give the public educational system the power to accomplish all this, in Talgo and Jarratt's opinion, the nature of education had to change—including government taking an increasingly active role in shaping the attitudes of succeeding generations.[19]

Talgo and Jarratt write, "The days in which parents and local governments determined the course of education policies have in many communities disappeared. Bureaucrats and lawmakers in state capitals and Washington, D.C. now issue edicts governing virtually everything, from what students eat for lunch to what they learn in history class."[20]

Because of this top-down federalized control of public education, curricula in public schools have been radically transformed. Parents and local communities have less and less say over what their children learn and how the school day is organized, to the point that many parents do not even consider they have a right to be more involved in determining the content and structure of their children's education. Today, many parents have no idea what is being taught on a day-to-day basis in their children's schools—sometimes by choice, but sometimes because school administrators deliberately withhold information about curricula, content, and morally formative school policies.

When parents do express a desire to be more involved in their children's education—recall, this is the best predictor of academic success—in some instances, the response of public education administrators is to attack such parents as meddling and manipulative.

While parents should not be doing their children's homework for them, for instance, there are sincere parents who only want the best for their children and for other children, as well, who are told they are denying their children the ability to think for themselves. The goal of the progressive education reformers of the past century was to shape attitudes and make children think for themselves, and not just engage in learning facts.

So, what can be done as "little platoons" to fix our nation's educational system?

Ultimately, restoring our nation's educational system starts at home. It requires parents to be emotionally and intellectually involved in their children's education. Parents need to interact with their children on a daily basis about what they are learning and what is going on in their schools. It does not mean constantly hovering over them or berating them and their teachers if they struggle, but it means encouraging them.

For some, the only solution remains more money rather than finding a way to repair families—which, in turn, should increase parental involvement—or to increase competition so underperforming schools, like businesses, have to improve or lose "customers." Many parents are finally seeing that they need to reclaim their children's education through other options, such as charter schools, that are accountable to parents while also requiring active parental participation.

Other options are private schools, of course, for those parents who can afford them. But for many families, that is not a possibility unless they have some form of government assistance, such as vouchers, tuition tax credits, or education savings accounts. That is a place where those who do not have children currently enrolled in school can help. There are multiple ways to support parents who are seeking a better education for their children.

One such example is in Arizona, where there is a tuition tax credit program that allows taxpayers to donate up to a certain amount for a specific child to an approved scholarship organization. The organization then provides a scholarship to a private or religious school of the parents' choice. The donor is able to write off the donation when they pay their annual state income tax. The tax credit can be used for any child, not just a family member, and is a great tool for churches and communities to help poorer parents or large families give their children access to better education. The tax credit program also supports good private schools not dependent upon government funding that are therefore more accountable to the parents of their students than to the federal government in curriculum and policy decisions. It also helps parents with special needs children who need extra assistance—such as Craig's neighbors, whose autistic son requires more attention than a public school system can provide and would be financially unable to send their son to the school he needs without this assistance. Craig and his wife used this program to help this young family.

The data are clear: when parents are allowed a greater say and involvement in their children's education, children thrive. But this leads us back to the fundamental problem we previously discussed. Marriage and family are in crisis in our nation today. Children cannot benefit from their parents' involvement in their education if there is no parent capable of being involved—either because the parent is absent or because a single parent is struggling to keep the home functioning on a basic level and does not have the time and mental space to be highly engaged in his or her child's education.

George Will perhaps put it best when he wrote, "the best predictor of a school's performance is the quality of the family life from which the children came." He states that this includes the quality and quantity of reading material children have access to in the home, the amount of electronic entertainment children are subjected to, the amount of homework performed there, and, in his words, "most important—the number of parents in the home." He concludes, "Family disintegration is the stubborn fact that severely limits the efficacy of even the best education policies."[21]

Ultimately, the restoration of education will require a rejuvenated national commitment to the renewal, preservation, and strengthening of families and parenting. This will occur through the strengthening of the bedrock institutions of marriage, community, church, and work. The Coleman Report deserves to be dusted off and its observations taken seriously as subsequent research continues to demonstrate the unbreakable relationship between the social stability of intact families and the upward mobility of the young people—upward mobility that will only occur through a quality education that prepares them to become the productive citizens of tomorrow.

CHAPTER NINE

Restoring Civility

"America's two great ideological tribes are in the midst of a similar conflict. It's the battle over civility, and all too often, reason, compassion, and grace are on the losing side." [1]

—David French, *National Review*

"Today, any disagreement on any issue means all-out war. Not mere ideological opposition, but all out moral and ethical warfare that necessitates humiliation, scare tactics, and reprehension." [2]

—Louis Sarkozy, the *Washington Examiner*

"If in 1970, a nerd slandered one on the sidewalk and talked trash, he might not do it twice; in 2018, he did electronically, boldly, and with impunity behind an array of masked social-media identities." [3]

—Victor Davis Hanson, *National Review*

"Democracy demands that we're able to also get inside the reality of people who are different than us, so we can understand their point of view. Maybe we can change their minds, maybe they'll change ours. You can't do this if you just out of hand disregard what your opponent has to say from the start." [4]

— former president Barack Obama

Arthur Brooks of the American Enterprise Institute shared about an incident he observed on the National Mall in September 2017 when a group called the Mother of All Rallies Patriot Unification Gathering, which supports President Donald

Trump, found itself in confrontation with a Black Lives Matter group from Greater New York.

What could have escalated into something very ugly did not. Why? Because the organizer of the pro-Trump rally, Tommy Gunn, invited the head of the Black Lives Matter group, Hawk Newsome, on to the stage and gave him two minutes to share his views, telling him, "We're going to give you two minutes of our platform to put your message out. Whether they disagree or agree with your message is irrelevant. It's the fact that you have the right to have the message."

After giving his message, the hostility disappeared and people applauded the person with whom they had previously sparred. While the two sides still disagreed on the issues, they had a newfound respect for each other. Brooks, a conservative, wrote, "Did the two sides reach agreement on policy or President Trump? Doubtlessly not. Yet something more profound happened: They saw each as people."[5] He concluded, "People are more hostile to others in the abstract than when they meet them in person."[6]

Unfortunately, when Americans do not interact with each other like this, natural biases take precedence, building up walls between our fellow citizens. This loss of civility and relationships is also lamented by some on the left side of the political spectrum. Richard Reeves of the left-leaning Brookings Institute wrote in *National Affairs* that American society was fragmenting. He, too, bemoaned the loss of mediating institutions such as churches, synagogues, unions, and social clubs, resulting in social gaps that cause Americans to interact more with people who are like them.[7]

Indianapolis Star columnist and cartoonist Gary Varvel concurs. He writes that politics for some people has become the new religion, on both the left and the right. And as a result, "we've decided to characterize those on the other side who don't agree with us as nonbelievers who don't deserve mercy or grace."[8]

At the 2004 Democratic National Convention, vice presidential nominee John Edwards spoke about his perception that in our nation there are "two Americas." His focus was on economic divisions, and there was some truth to his "Two Americas" theme on those issues—especially when one looks at the plight of areas such as the Appalachians compared to wealthy metropolises on the coasts.[9]

However, Edwards was incomplete in his analysis. There are several other ways beyond economics in which two Americas exist with citizens of each holding wildly different opinions on issues. Sadly, it seems in recent years that each side of the divide has increasing antipathy for the other.

A 2017 Pew Research poll found "among members of both [political] parties, the shares with very unfavorable opinions of the other party have more than doubled since 1994."[10] Forty-four percent of Democrats said they had a very unfavorable opinion of Republicans, and 45 percent of Republicans felt the same way about Democrats.[11]

Writing in the *Hill*, Lara Brown, associate professor and director of the Graduate School of Political Management at George Washington University, observed, "Republicans and Democrats don't want to live in the same types of communities and most admit they have 'very few or no' friends on the other side of the aisle."[12] Americans are not only not engaging with each other, but they are avoiding each other like the plague with the national media dividing them into "red" and "blue" states at war with each other.

But there was one issue nearly all could agree on: 80 percent of all voters believe America is a divided country.[13] Democratic Party pollster Fred Yang commented, "It's as if everyone agrees that it's too divisive and we can't get along, but also that everyone else is wrong."[14]

Commenting on that survey, Janet Hook of the *Journal* wrote, "political divisions are now especially hard to bridge. People who identify with either party increasingly disagree not just on policy; they inhabit separate worlds of differing social and cultural values and even see their economic outlook through partisan eyes."[15]

This has all led to many speculating whether or not a new civil war is on the horizon, or, in the words of political scientist Thomas Schaller, "I think we're at the beginning of a soft civil war…I don't know if the country gets out of it whole."[16]

An article in the *New York Times* documented this "soft" civil war. Some of the examples cited were a Georgia couple, married for two decades, who have pretty much stopped speaking to each other over politics; a teenager wearing a "Make America Great Again" hat having his hat ripped off his head and a drink thrown in his face while eating at a fast food restaurant; and a mother needing to get professional conflict mediators to intervene when her two daughters refused to speak to each other over the holidays because of their political differences.[17]

Pollster Frank Luntz confirmed this animosity between friends and family. He surveyed one thousand voters on ninety-six questions and found nearly one-third said they stopped talking to a friend or family member because of political disagreements.[18] Carolyn Lukens-meyer, executive director of the National Institute for Civil Discourse, says, "This is now deep in our homes, deep in our neighborhoods, and deep in our workplaces. It really is a virus."[19]

A June 2018 Rasmussen poll found 31 percent of likely U.S. voters said it was likely the United States would undergo a second civil war in their lifetime, with 11 percent saying it was very likely. In addition, 59 percent of all voters were concerned that those opposed to policies of the current administration would resort to violence, with 33 percent very concerned.[20]

A few months later, a survey done by John Zogby Strategies found 39 percent of the population supported the right for states to secede from the union. The poll reported, "Overall support for secession remains only twelve points from a majority." The desire to secede was strongest among Democrats, with 42 percent supporting secession. Among African Americans, 47 percent now support secession.[21]

As Glenn Harlan Reynolds, law professor at the University of Tennessee, warns, "Marriage counselors say that when a couple views one another with contempt, it's a top indicator that the relationship is likely to fail. Americans, who used to know how to disagree with one another without being mutually contemptuous, seem to be forgetting this."[22]

One of the most acute areas of this divide can been seen on cultural issues, as evidenced in the findings of a 2017 *Wall Street Journal–NBC News* social trends survey. The survey reported 42 percent of Republicans believe marriage is the union of one man and one woman, compared to only 17 percent of Democrats. For Democrats, 77 percent are comfortable with social changes such as abortion and same-sex marriage. In contrast, only 30 percent of Republicans are.[23] This may be because Democrats are twice as likely never to attend church as their GOP counterparts,[24] and therefore far more apt to have secular beliefs on issues.

Sadly, in many instances, the coastal states—a.k.a. the "blue" states—have nothing but contempt for the values of Middle America and the South—a.k.a. the "red" states—and vice versa. People living in the San Francisco Bay Area seethe in anger over the values of their fellow citizens in most of Middle America and the South while many living in Middle America and the South have a hard time hiding their contempt for the values of the so-called "Left Coast."

Hoover Institution fellow Victor Davis Hanson wrote that, in his view, America is nearing a point comparable with 1860—the start of the Civil War—and perhaps past 1968—the combustible year that saw the tragic assassinations of Rev. Martin Luther King Jr. and Robert Kennedy, along with massive anti-war protests across the country. He says, "Left-right factionalism is increasingly fueled by geography—always history's force multiplier of civil strife. Red and blue states ensure that locale magnifies differences that were mostly manageable during the administrations of Ford, Carter, Reagan, the Bushes, and Clinton." [25]

This became evident in 2016 when the presidential nominee for one political party went as far as to describe those who supported her opponent and disagreed with her views as "deplorables" and "irredeemable." [26] She lumped ordinary Americans who believe in biblical standards for sexual morality or had differing views from her and her supporters on issues such as illegal immigration, abortion, and the environment with truly repugnant behaviors, such as racism.

Her comment confirmed in the minds of many Americans how many of their fellow citizens felt this about them. When one sees those with whom one disagrees as "deplorable," "hateful," or "bigoted" simply for having a different, but legitimate, viewpoint, the possibility of civil discourse quickly dissipates.

Louis Sarkozy, son of the former French President Nicolas Sarkozy, perhaps put it best when he wrote:

> This strategy of demonization is quite an effective one. It brands anyone in disagreement with you on any topic hateful and bigoted and by doing so automatically grants you the high moral ground…when the name-calling begins, it is almost impossible for it to be retracted, and any sort of rational, intellectual debate is thrown out the window. [27]

This was not the intent of the Founding Fathers, who were fully aware of the potential effect of incivility on the new country they helped create. After the debate and vote on the U.S. Constitution, a woman asked Benjamin Franklin, "Well, Doctor, what have we got—A republic or a monarchy?" about what he and the other Founders had just done. He famously replied, "A republic, if you can keep it." [28]

What Franklin and the other Founders hoped to create was a thriving constitutional republic in which citizens engaged in lively debate with each other about the common good, but still retained the ability to put aside their differences for the preservation of the nation.

American citizens have displayed this spirit during times of national crisis. In World War II, Democrats and Republicans put aside their partisan differences and worked together to defeat the Axis powers. In the days shortly after September 11, 2001, we saw the same spirit at work.

This type of basic civility is rooted in a kind of simple, elemental courtesy best described by C. S. Lewis in *Mere Christianity* when he wrote that courtesy is the idea "that no one give any kind of preference to himself." He said the practice of courtesy in the public square was on the achievements of a "fully Christian society." Unfortunately, the current state of our civil discourse reflects the exact opposite of what Lewis described.

Americans have also struggled throughout our history with the issue of civility, and the divisions we see today are not new. The founding of the United States of America turned on a fulcrum of massive disagreement on numerous significant issues, including whether to have a permanent or impermanent national military, whether each state should have its own money or whether there should be a national currency, and whether to spread or limit slavery. In 1856, on the floor of the U.S. Congress, anti-slavery Senator Charles Sumner of Massachusetts bled profusely and nearly died after being attacked with a cane by pro-slavery Representative Preston Brooks of South Carolina.[29]

There are countless examples of Americans acting uncivilly to each other, and there is no denying the reality that in the midst of the discussions, some grievous decisions occurred—specifically the decision to allow the practice of slavery to continue within the United States. That decision almost destroyed our nation, resulting in bloody conflict that cost the lives of thousands of men. It also continues to haunt us to this day, as many of the wounds between the North and South still exist more than 150 years later.

While there has always been some form of incivility in American culture, the Internet—with the subsequent rise of social media—has been like throwing gasoline on a fire. The result has been an alarming rise in uncivil behavior toward our fellow citizens. This lack of civility is present on both the Left and the Right, with each side pointing fingers at the other. Both sides view their positions as absolutes with no room for compromise and therefore have no tolerance for each other's views. They are instead opposing parties seeking to silence, punish, and in some cases criminalize—and perhaps even murder—those they perceive to be their adversaries.

Perhaps the scariest example of the current breakdown in civility happened in 2017 when a shooter opened fire on several members of the Republican Party practicing for their annual baseball game against the Democrats. The shooter, James Hodgkinson, asked if the people practicing were Republicans. When he learned they were, he opened fire, gravely wounding then–House Majority Whip Steve Scalise (who fortunately survived the shooting). Had it not been for the members of the Capitol Hill Police who were on site to protect Scalise as a high-ranking member of the government, many more members of Congress could have been shot.[30] While assassinations and other politically motivated murders have tragically occurred throughout human history, this attack was symbolic of what happens when civil discourse degrades to the point where it leads a person to attack physically those with whom he disagrees.

While this is perhaps the most extreme example, the list of ways Americans are acting in an uncivil manner toward each other is seemingly endless. For example, after the last presidential election, some websites began posting content advocating for *increased* incivility and encouraging people, especially young people, to heighten the tension about politics within their own families and communities.

As mentioned earlier, incivility has crept into family relationships. Around the holidays in 2016 and 2017, *GQ* magazine, the Huffington Post, and the Establishment ran articles including talking points about specific ways for people to use Thanksgiving and Christmas dinners to confront and humiliate family members who hold different political views. Rather than encouraging people to look beyond politics to find points of commonality, these cultural influencers and leaders set out deliberately to exacerbate tensions by turning the holidays—times when Americans traditionally come together to enjoy family, put aside their differences, and give thanks to God—into an opportunity to engage in angry partisan warfare.[31]

Joe Berkowitz, writing in *GQ*, suggested that those who do not support President Trump should not offer a handshake to their family members who do. In his words, they should "just stare, disgustedly, at their outstretched arms." He goes on to say they should treat their parents—if they support the president—with disdain. He advocates that they refuse to be alone in a room with their mother, because Vice President Mike Pence will never meet one on one with another woman besides his wife. He finally recommends they should call their parents by mocking nicknames associated with the president.[32] Thus, you have the example cited earlier of the mother who had to consult with conflict mediators to get her daughters to talk with each other again.

Some of these same groups say they want civility, but it quickly becomes evident they only want it on their terms—which means total surrender to their worldview. David French wrote about this for *National Review* in 2018, saying:

> Calls for civility are often one-sided, manipulative, and made in bad faith. It turns out that each ideological tribe is

often quite tolerant of the vicious voices on its own side and positively *repulsed* by anger in response. You see the double standard all the time. The same people who lament the angry voices on Fox News or talk radio will positively thrill to the latest Michael Moore documentary.... [33]

To be fair, it is not just the political Left engaging in such activity. One only needs to read the comments section on conservative websites to see the utter disdain toward those of a progressive bent. To use French's words, you can make the same case that those who lament the angry progressive voices on CNN or MSNBC positively thrill to the latest documentary bashing those opinions.

This raises the question: Can a constitutional republic last and thrive when many Americans cannot stand the sight of each other?

The answer, despite the historical and present evidence, is "yes." Civil discourse is not something that takes place far away from us, over which we have no control. Rather, it starts with us—with how we think about and act toward each other. Therefore, our national healing also begins with us—the individual men and women who make up American society.

We who are part of the Body of Christ have a special role to play. This is because bringing healing must begin with changing how we perceive our neighbors—both those who agree with us and those who disagree with us. We cannot view people as members of warring tribes, either "for" us or "against" us. Rather, we must view them as unique representations of the image of God and realize every interaction we have with one another is an opportunity to honor and uphold that image. A superficial "niceness" is not what we are striving for; what we must pursue is the constant recognition of God's presence through the people around us. As the late Chuck Colson said, "the virtue of courtesy is rooted in the idea of the *imago Dei*, the concept that each of us was created in the image of a loving God. That is what gives each person—every person—dignity and make each of us worthy of respect." [34]

When we do not recognize the dignity of every person, it becomes easy to dismiss, demonize, and dehumanize people. As Christians, we are called to see people as God sees them, extending grace to those with whom we disagree. Thus, we must be models of civility not just to our fellow brothers and sisters in Christ, but to everyone with whom we come into contact—beginning with our words and actions toward those who seek to silence us, shout us down, and persecute us.

Brit Hume, a committed Christian and former White House correspondent, perhaps put it best when he said America needs to follow "Step 10" from the "Big Book of Alcoholics Anonymous," which states, "Nothing pays off like restraint on pen and tongue." [35]

This is particularly true with social media, which has become a cesspool of incivility toward our fellow man. Perhaps the first place to start restoring a culture of civility is to resist the temptation to respond in kind on social media when we or our beliefs are attacked.

As the Apostle James wrote, "[The tongue] is a restless evil, full of deadly poison. With it, we bless our Lord and Father, and with it, we curse people who are made in the likeness of God. From the same mouth, come blessing and cursing. My brothers, these things ought not to be so" (James 3:8–10 ESV).

The angry words we type in a social media post are just an extension of our tongue as they reflect what is in our hearts. If we are cursing people made in the likeness of God, in our hearts, we are, in a way, cursing God, as well.

In these contentious times, it is easy for us to forget this admonishment. As a result, we end up acting and speaking like the rest of mankind, expressing condemnation instead of grace, anger instead of patience, and hatred instead of love.

Civility, however, does not require us to allow others to walk over us, nor does it prevent us from defending what we believe to be the truth. As Chuck Colson said, "Out of honor for the God we worship, we should—we must—refuse to be silenced." We are called to be "salt and light"—to speak the Truth in love. The key is *in love*—with a combination of civility, diplomacy, grace, and without apology—in that order.

Victor Davis Hanson of the Hoover Institution perhaps put it best when he wrote:

> "Religious and spiritual reawakening is crucial [to restore civility]. The master of the universe of Silicon Valley did not, as promised, bring us new-age tranquility, but rather only greater speed and intensity to do what we always do. Trolling, doxing, and phishing were just new versions of what Jesus warned about in the Sermon on the Mount." [36]

Perhaps one of the best summaries of all this was provided by Gary Varvel, who offers three suggestions for handing those who oppose our views. They are words of wisdom by which we should all abide. He suggests we must control our emotions and refuse to give in to the dark side, treat people the way we want to be treated, and when wronged, give grace and forgiveness to those who harmed us.[37]

Louis Sarkozy concurs, writing that we should gravitate toward disagreement and attacks and counter them with a kind heart and firm intellect instead of running from them and only surrounding ourselves with those with whom we agree.[38]

An example of someone who follows these suggestions is our good friend and colleague Glenn Stanton. Glenn is an unapologetic defender of marriage and speaks passionately about the negative consequences for society when that institution is weakened.

But Glenn's passion is matched by the dignity and grace he extends to those who oppose him. Thus, while many of his opponents may vehemently disagree with his faith-based opinion, they have come to love and respect Glenn as a person, and vice versa—opening opportunities for dialogue that might not have existed otherwise. As a result, Glenn, while still standing for eternal Truth, can engage with them in the type of civil discourse the Founders had in mind when they created this constitutional republic. Glenn understands what *imago Dei* is all about, to which his life is a testament. There are still some who seek to defame Glenn, but when those moments come, it is often his opponents who come to his defense.

If we are to recover and restore civility in the public square, we need again to realize and live out the truth that each and every man, woman, and child is made in the image of God. That remarkable reality gives men and women of faith a responsibility to follow Christ's example of Christian charity toward their neighbors, regardless of their views.

The world, despite its expressed antipathy toward people of faith, ultimately looks to us to see how we will respond during these times. If we respond with anger, they will respond accordingly. If we respond with love, while they may be initially resistant, our response will help plant a seed of reconciliation and brotherhood that can bridge whatever political and ideological chasms exist between us.

A famous example from recent history is the relationship of then-President Ronald Reagan and Speaker of the House Tip O'Neill. Even though they were entrenched political opponents during the day, Tip O'Neill's son Thomas recalled that while they disagreed vehemently with each other, they respected each other's right to hold the view they did.

When Ronald Reagan was nearly assassinated at the Washington Hilton in 1981, Tip O'Neill went to his hospital room to pray for his fallen ideological opponent. Ronald Reagan helped raise one million dollars to build the O'Neill Library at Boston College. Thomas O'Neill wrote, "While neither man embraced the other's worldview, each respected the other's right to hold it. Each respected the other as a man."[39]

In a recent piece Republican Harry J. Kazianis, executive editor of the *National Interest*, and Democratic public relations executive Neal Urwitz share not just the O'Neill-Reagan story but also about the friendship of two former senators: conservative Republican Bob Smith of New Hampshire and liberal Ted Kennedy of Massachusetts. While they disagreed on practically every issue, they were good friends and found ways to work together on issues important to the country.

Kazianis and Urwitz write, "America does better when two sides of the aisle talk to each other, respect each other, and even like each other. America does best when Americans recognize that people from the other party still want what's best for the nation—they just have a different route to get there." They conclude that what is holding us back on critical issues—such as repairing America's crumbling infrastructure, broken educational system, and a host of other issues—isn't the issues themselves, but the vitriol of our political discourse.

They conclude:

> We can only take on the issues we all agree on when we tamp down our rhetoric and see the good in each other ... America has become an angry place, a place where demonizing the other side has become the rule. But that anger needs to stop. We must put down our vicious tweets and blog posts and pick up a six-pack or a cup of coffee with someone of a different political persuasion. We might actually find out we like each other, and we ... might do some good for the country we love.[40]

If we, as people of faith, can act in a civil manner and resist the temptation to respond in kind to those who attack us, we can become friends with those who oppose us—no matter how much we disagree. Yes, there will always be those who will not accept that olive branch and will continue to attack us, regardless of how nice we are. But that does not mean we should cease our efforts to act civilly; nor does it mean we need to compromise our beliefs just to get along.

As Arthur Brooks concluded after watching the incident on the National Mall, "Be like Tommy Gunn, and without repudiating your own views, invite the 'other' on to your stage. Be like Hawk Newsome and go where people are hostile and tell them what is in your heart."[41]

Finally, we must always remember that regardless of how strong our political sentiments may be, our identity is in Christ, and not in politics. Moreover, because our identity is in Christ, we must treat those with whom we disagree with respect.

While there may be two Americas—often with very divergent views—we can once again become the constitutional republic the Founding Fathers sought to create: a republic that engages in robust debate, but never forgets the human dignity of those with whom we disagree.

CHAPTER TEN

Restoring Citizenship and Duty

"The exercise of rights is justified only if the claimant of rights stands ready to fulfill the corresponding duties." [1]
—Russell Kirk

"A people that values its privileges above its principles soon loses both." [2]
—Dwight D. Eisenhower

"Lastly, our ancestors established their system of government on morality and religious sentiment. Moral habits, they believed, cannot safely be trusted on any other foundation than religious principle, nor any government be secure which is not supported by moral habits.... Whatever makes men good Christians, makes them good citizens..." [3]
—Daniel Webster

"Ask not what your country can do for you, but what you can do for your country." [4]
—Orestes Brownson

I n 2016, Supreme Court Justice Clarence Thomas delivered the commencement address to graduates at Hillsdale College in Michigan. While many speakers use commencement addresses to boost graduates' confidence with lofty platitudes about following one's dreams or believing in one's potential, Justice Thomas chose to go a different route.

He spoke not about what the world has to offer young people, but instead what they ought to offer the world. He emphasized to the graduates that as they entered the public square, they must be aware of what it means to be an American citizen; citizenship, he told them, is a duty—not a privilege.

Justice Thomas titled his speech "Freedom and Obligation." For its clear-eyed grasp of timeless truths and its trenchant applicability to daily life, it—along with John F. Kennedy's inaugural address and Ronald Reagan's farewell address—deserves to be part of the canon of contemporary political writing on what it means to be a great citizen. It is a template for the restoration of the idea of model citizenship, going to the core of what it means to be a citizen in a constitutional republic like America.

Justice Thomas asserts that in keeping with a long philosophical tradition, the reverse side of freedom is responsibility; there is a vital relationship between the liberty of a thriving constitutional republic and the day-to-day duty and sacrifice of individual citizens. In his view—which draws on ancient and medieval ideas of freedom, as well as the finest of Enlightenment political thought—liberty comes with deep and abiding obligations.

The most important of these obligations, Thomas says, is to live with integrity and responsibility—virtues often expressed in small and unrecognized ways, such as being a good neighbor, a dedicated employee, a committed church member, or an engaged member of the community. Living a life of integrity means being true to our values and ourselves while keeping our commitments to others and to ourselves. One of the key elements of living a life of integrity is having what can be best called an "attitude of gratitude." In the words of Tom Ziglar, son of the late famous motivational speaker Zig Ziglar, "those who are grateful for what they have, even if it's not much, are more likely to make good, sound, ethical and moral decisions based on what is right."[5]

Justice Thomas echoed these thoughts in his speech, stating that a good citizen is one who takes personal responsibility for his or her actions, who puts the needs of others before his or her own, who is grateful for the blessings he or she has received, and who believes in shared sacrifice for the greater good.

There have been times in American history where we have seen this type of citizenship in full bloom. As discussed in the chapter on civility, Americans put aside their differences and joined in mutual and serious sacrifice to defeat the Axis powers and preserve freedom. Americans were grateful for the God-given freedom bequeathed by our nation's founders. Out of this shared gratitude, they came together as one. Millions of men were willing to sacrifice their lives, and millions of women gave up their husbands, sons, brothers, and way of life so others could continue to experience that freedom.

However, because we are all sinners, people have struggled with gratitude, integrity, and personal responsibility going back to the Garden of Eden. That struggle seems to be particularly acute today as it becomes more and more commonplace to put privileges over principles. The loss of gratitude has had a corrosive effect on our national unity.

Rather than being grateful for what they have received, many Americans continue to make demands for more and more special benefits. Personal entitlement has replaced an attitude of gratitude, creating a society where individuals' perceived "needs" are more important than a collective sense of responsibility to our fellow citizens.

Thus, the national debt—which is at nearly twenty-two trillion dollars and growing[6]—explodes to pay for new government programs to meet these demands, resulting in a vicious cycle that will eventually cripple the financial outlook for future generations. Demands of special interest groups' agendas that are being taught in public schools instead of fundamental basics such as reading, writing, civics, math, and science rob children of the skills they need to succeed in life. As a result, society becomes a runaway train that will eventually crash when the bills come due for these benefits or when its citizenry can no longer compete with those of other nations.

As Dwight Eisenhower warned in his 1953 inaugural speech, when this happens, both privileges and principles are in jeopardy.

It is tempting to look for the source of this breakdown in political leaders, Hollywood, the media, and other national-level institutions. But the problem starts not on the federal level, but on the local level in our communities and homes. As Aleksandr Solzhenitsyn wrote in *The Gulag Archipelago*, "the line between good and evil runs through every human heart."[7] We must trace the source of both virtue and vice not to others or to societal pressures, but to the decisions and choices we make in the secret places of our own souls because those decisions have ramifications on every level of society.

For instance, gratitude is not something to be taught in a public school. It is something caught, and the catching of gratitude starts in the home. Jennifer Breheny Wallace, writing in the *Wall Street Journal*, documents her observations of how gratitude (citizenship with it) has lessened while a sense of personal entitlement has increased, especially among the young. Wallace writes, "Every generation seems to complain that children 'these days' are so much more entitled and ungrateful than in years past. This time, they may be right. In today's selfie culture, which often rewards bragging and arrogance over kindness and humility, many people are noticing a drop-off in everyday expressions of gratitude."[8]

One woman she interviewed said she has noticed a distinct lack of the most basic elements of gratitude and even the most basic of manners among her sons' peers to the point of rudeness. Young people, she says, do not use even simple mannerly gestures such as looking adults in the eye to thank them. Parents, Wallace writes, have become so demoralized by their children's behavior they do not even expect their children to be thankful anymore.

Wallace's report is not offtrack. A 2012 national online poll of two thousand adults commissioned by the John Templeton Foundation backed up her observations. The poll found 59 percent of those surveyed felt most people today are "less likely to have an attitude of gratitude than 10 or 20 years ago." Most alarming is that the youngest group (ages 18–24) were the least likely to report expressing gratitude on a regular basis (just 35 percent) and the most likely to engage in self-serving reasons for expressing gratitude, saying that being grateful will "encourage people to be kind and generous to me." [9]

Gratitude cannot arise in a metaphysical vacuum. It is difficult to be grateful when one believes one is merely the product of random forces at work in the universe, that there is no direction or purpose to one's life, and that one's whole existence is an accident. In a 2011 study on gratitude, Dr. David Rosmarin, director of the Spirituality and Mental Health Program at McLean Hospital in Belmont, Massachusetts, and assistant professor of psychiatry at Harvard University, found faith in God is an essential element in gratitude. He says, "Gratitude is a spiritual emotion, whether it's implicitly or explicitly expressed." [10]

For the study, which was published in the *Journal of Positive Psychology*, researchers working with Rosmarin assessed the gratitude, religious commitment, and mental and physical well-being of more than four hundred adults surveyed online. They found that grateful individuals had less anxiety and depression, as well as greater well-being. Significantly, they found a correlation between gratitude and religious commitment, with many of the more grateful people saying that they were grateful to God. These individuals showed lower levels of anxiety and depression, as well as increased personal well-being. [11]

Although the spiritual condition of the human heart is a primary reason why we have seen a breakdown in citizenship, there are other factors in play, as well. It is hard for someone to be an involved and knowledgeable citizen when he does not even know the most basic aspects of how our government—and consequently our society—works.

Stephen Macedo, professor of politics and director of the University Center for Human Values at Princeton University, writes that until the 1960s it was common for high school students to take as many as three courses in civics, democracy, and government. Now, they take only one such course. He adds, the National Assessment of Education Progress only assesses civic knowledge every ten years. He states, "This sends the signal that civic education matters very little."[12]

As a result, many students are graduating from high school not knowing the basics of how our government works. A 2006 Zogby poll found nearly three-quarters of high school students asked could identify Moe, Larry, and Curly as the Three Stooges, but only 42 percent were able to name the legislative, executive, and judicial branches of government. In addition, another Zogby poll discovered that 77 percent of Americans could name two of the seven dwarves from Snow White, but only 24 percent could name two of the nine Supreme Court justices.[13]

Perhaps even more alarming was a survey done by the Freedom Forum on the "State of the First Amendment." The results were disturbing. More than 1,000 people were surveyed, and only one—just one—person was able to name all five First Amendment rights. Forty percent could not recall any of the First Amendment freedoms, and only 3 percent could name four out of the five. The most remembered right was freedom of speech at 56 percent, and only 15 percent identified freedom of religion.[14] These polls and surveys are sad commentaries on the state of America's civic knowledge.

Without even the most basic knowledge about how our government works, it comes as no surprise that Americans are participating in the democratic process less and less. In 1972, about half of those between the ages of eighteen and twenty-nine voted in the presidential election. By 1996, that percentage decreased to approximately one-third.[15]

While voter turnout tends to increase with age, America remains still well below many other wealthy nations in general in this area. The Pew Research Center compiled recent voter turnout data for developed countries from the International Institute for Democracy and Electoral Assistance (IIDEA) and found the United States clearly lagged behind other wealthy nations when it came to turnout. The United States ranked thirty-first among the thirty-five countries in the Organization for Economic Cooperation and Development.[16] Despite the lack of civic knowledge—which is lamentable and needs to be addressed—the key to becoming a good citizen still rests with each of us.

In his Hillsdale address, Justice Thomas concluded that instead of trying to dedicate their lives to change the world, students should instead begin to practice responsibility, dignity, and gratitude in their own lives. Instead of fixating on implementing sweeping social changes from the top down, they should first examine how they treat those closest to them.

Leo Tolstoy warned against the temptation to try to fix society without taking responsibility for oneself, saying, "And yet in our world everybody thinks of changing humanity, and nobody thinks of changing himself." [17] Justice Thomas argued in his speech that this kind of personal moral responsibility—the mundane drama of trying to change oneself, played out on the smallest and least glamorous of stages—is what America's Founders believed could make the free society they envisioned possible. He said:

> As you go through life, try to be a person whose actions teach others how to be better people and better citizens. Reach out to the shy person who is not so popular. Stand up for others when they're being treated unfairly. Take the time

to listen to the friend who's having a difficult time. Do not hide your faith and beliefs under a bushel basket, especially in this world that seems to have gone mad with political correctness.[18]

The first step in becoming a great citizen is acquiring an attitude of gratitude—similar to the one displayed by Abraham Lincoln when he addressed Congress in his first State of the Union address as the nation crumbled around him. Despite the incredible domestic turmoil, Lincoln still expressed gratitude to God for "unusual good health and abundant harvests."[19]

Secondly parents play a critical role in establishing an attitude of gratitude in their children. Kathleen Cormier, a mother from Minneapolis, Minnesota, seeks to do just this. Ever since her children were little, she has worked diligently to develop such an attitude in her children. The result is that showing gratitude comes naturally to them. Cormier encourages gratitude for "everyday stuff" by example. If one of her children holds a door open for her or notices the trash is full and takes it out, she thanks them. As a result, she says, "my kids thank me every single time I put fresh sheets on their bed, make them dinner, or do some other act that for many mothers goes unnoticed."[20] By teaching our children to be grateful toward others and for the blessings they have received, we are helping them become thoughtful and thankful adults.

Finally, besides teaching children to be grateful, parents cannot assume their children will receive what they need to be informed citizens at school. Dinnertime conversations about current events or sharing stories from history can often spark a child's interest and provide him or her with the opportunity to think critically about issues. In his earlier mentioned 1989 farewell address to the nation, then-President Ronald Reagan perhaps put it best when he said, "All great change in America begins at the dinner table."[21]

He added, "An informed patriotism is what we want.... We've got to teach history based not on what's in fashion, but what's important—why the Pilgrims came here, who Jimmy Doolittle was, and what those 30 seconds over Tokyo meant.... If we forget what we did, we won't know who we are." [22]

Parents can model citizenship to their children through engaging in joint service projects to benefit the community. Instilling personal and corporate responsibility helps children see the world is far more than just themselves.

An informed and grateful citizenry that puts aside political differences, sees their friends and neighbors as bearing the image of God, and comes together in times of great need—whether it be a world war, a devastating hurricane, or some other catastrophic event—will go a long way in America's restoration.

These are the men and women who invite people from all walks of life into their homes for dinner, who open their furniture store to feed displaced people and provide them a place to sleep, and who adopt needy children when they cannot have children of their own. They are lovers of country, but more importantly, lovers of their fellow brothers and sisters.

These are people with integrity and responsibility that spring from a grateful heart. They are "citizens."

CHAPTER ELEVEN

Restoring Community

"One of the most destructive problems is the breakdown of community, and it is this breakdown that has often led to the breakdown of persons. Though we may put many around us, we are alone.... We do not concern ourselves much with the plight of others except a few we may call family or friends, and even then, our concern and attention is [sic] waning." [1]

—Dan Edmunds, Diplomate of the American Psychotherapy Association

"One man's life touches so many others, when he's not there, it leaves an awfully big hole." [2]

— *It's a Wonderful Life*

"Americans of all ages, all conditions, and all dispositions constantly form associations. They have not only commercial and manufacturing associations, in which all partake, but associations of a thousand other kinds—religious, moral, serious, futile, general or restricted, enormous or diminutive. Wherever at the head of some new undertaking you see the government of France, or a man of rank in England, in the United States you will be sure to find an association." [3]

—Alexis de Tocqueville, *Democracy in America*

A fter attending the 2018 Super Bowl between the New England Patriots and the Philadelphia Eagles, Ben Shapiro noticed that while the people in the stadium may have hated the other team, they did not hate each other. Patriots fans sat next to Eagles fans and everybody got along, despite their divided loyalties.

Shapiro points out:

> We all shouted ourselves hoarse when the NFL honored Medal of Honor winners, and we all stood for the national anthem. After the game, when we poured out into the arctic temperatures, barely able to move because of the throng, nobody was pushing or shoving or getting violent. Instead, people joked and laughed.... We'd just witnessed an awesome spectacle, been party to a shared communal experience.... It may sound like a cliché, but the Super Bowl—in the stadium, at least—was just a giant party filled with Americans who loved being in America celebrating a great American cultural celebration.[4]

Unfortunately, Shapiro notes such experiences are becoming rarer and rarer.

He goes on to lament the increased fragmentation of American society and the loss of community and a shared sense of citizenship. He sees many reasons for this increasing fragmentation. For Shapiro, the central communal connections of his life come through his synagogue. But, as he observes, in recent years, church and synagogue attendance have dropped dramatically and the flight from religion shows no signs of slowing. He adds that people are not joining sports leagues or community organizations, another erstwhile source of community. Instead, more and more people are staying home behind locked doors as the Internet makes it possible for them to access more and more entertainment and shopping options without leaving the house. Just as shopping malls became the new town squares in the 1970s and 1980s, those malls where people gathered and interacted with others are now disappearing, as well. American life presents fewer and fewer opportunities to interact with other people and be exposed to differing viewpoints while remaining friends. People still have an emotional need for others, but it is increasingly unmet.

Several years ago, writing in the *Washington Times*, Christy Stutzman observed how neighbors never talk to each other. She asked, "How long has it been since we took a step back from our busy lives and made a genuine effort to be more engaged with those who live and work around us?" She asked whether the hostility so prevalent in America today would exist if neighbors were not strangers to one another.[5]

Shapiro goes one step further, writing that not only do we not see other people as friends or neighbors, but we no longer see one another even as potential friends or neighbors. Instead, we see each other as potential antagonists and we interact with those who disagree with us as nefarious characters, rather than just as friends or family with a different perspective.

Shapiro's and Stutzman's observations are not merely based in anecdotal observations. Statistics show Americans are, in fact, increasingly becoming strangers to each other—including within their neighborhoods. In 1974, 30 percent of Americans interacted with their neighbors once a week and just 20 percent said they never spoke with those who live around them. A 2017 survey found that almost 35 percent of Americans never interact with their neighbors and less than 20 percent speak with their neighbors on a weekly basis. Meanwhile, loneliness rates have more than doubled since the 1980s, rising from 20 to 40 percent.[6]

For millennials, the situation is even worse. A 2018 study found that 64 percent of millennials feel disconnected from their community. Compared with older generations, nearly twice as many millennials said they did not have time to participate in their local community by being part of civic groups, churches, synagogues, or even having get-togethers with their neighbors. In fact, 22 percent said they did not participate because they were not friends with anyone in their neighborhood, and 27 percent said they did not know how to make friends with their neighbors.

However, millennials are very much involved in online communities. Nearly 43 percent of millennials said they feel their online interactions suffice for their community needs, implying young people are increasingly more comfortable interacting via computer screen than in person.[7]

However, online interactions and groups are not an adequate substitute for live interactions. They tend to divide people into homogenous ideologically aligned groups; such groups do not provide the vital, sustained, face-to-face interaction with people of different perspectives and opinions so necessary for vibrant, honest relationships and common respect to develop. Overreliance on Internet relationships and communities results not in friendships, but in increased isolation and intolerance, generating more suspicion than trust in the human beings around us.

Peter Lovenheim writes about this increased isolation in his book *In the Neighborhood: The Search for Community on an American Street, One Sleepover at a Time.* He writes that there are numerous reasons for neighbors to no longer interact with each other. He cites the rise in two-career couples, which means people are not home during the day to interact with those around them. In addition, people spend more and more time in front of the television or on the internet. Finally, he says, in the suburbs lot and house sizes have nearly doubled since the 1950s. Thus, the distance between neighbors has increased.[8]

Older ideas of community were based on proximity; a community was a group of people who lived, worked, played, and worshipped with or near each other. Whether those people agreed, or even liked each other, was beside the point. Their physical proximity was enough to draw them into a meaningful relationship with each other. Today, however, we are far less bound to physical proximity in our lives. Most Americans live in car-dependent towns or cities, and as a result their lives are spread out across a massive area with home, work, school, and church all being several miles (at least) away—often in opposite directions.

Combine this with the intrusion of the Internet into every area of our lives, and the older perspective on community becomes unthinkable. For modern Americans, "community" increasingly means our tribe—the group of people we have self-selected to spend our free time with. This tribe usually consists of people quite similar to us in many ways: economically, politically, spiritually, and in age and stage of life. If our neighbors, or even our family members, differ from us substantially in any of these areas, it is both easy and acceptable to exclude them from our day-to-day lives and seek instead the company of those who are more like us.

This attitude has leaked into even the few remaining communal institutions, such as churches, service clubs, and other public and private associations. For example, rather than a church being a single community of believers who gather to participate in common worship, many churches now break people into different age groups. This fragmentation is well-intended, the belief being that people will benefit from meeting their peers. But the unintended consequence is that people never have to interact with someone younger or older than themselves. The wisdom that older generations can provide to younger, the enthusiasm and energy younger generations can share with older, the joy from sharing life with people who are at different stages—all these things are lost.

As community breaks down, people take refuge in either staunch individualism or fierce tribalism. Individualism in its worst form is the simple belief that life is essentially about oneself, and a happy life is one in which a person has as few obligations to other people as possible.

Tribalism, on the other hand, is "loyalty to a tribe or other social group especially when combined with strong negative feelings for people outside the group."[9] These two philosophies of life can be combined, so that a person can be part of a tribe that emphasizes individual expression and believes the good life comes from being free from restrictions or obligations.

In fact, French philosopher Pascal Bruckner has written that excessive individualism eventually leads to tribalism. Individualism releases people from their social obligations, resulting in their only being concerned about themselves or the members of their "tribe" with whom they feel comfortable. The tragedy of this individualistic tribalism, Bruckner says, is that while people may gain perceived freedom, they lose any sense of security.[10]

Writing in *National Review,* author Fred Bauer says tribalism is a "poor substitute for community." He writes, "Whereas the tribalist seeks grounds for belonging to a purified group, a member of a community accepts both human difference and commonality." This ability to accept human difference fostered by genuine community lends a sense of security; if we are able to love those who are different from us, we can hold out hope they will love us, as well. But if, from the midst of our homogenous tribe, we disdain and fear those who are different from us, of course we find ourselves assuming they disdain and fear us, as well.

As a result, when communities disintegrate and tribalism takes over, it leads to societal fragmentation as people return to what they perceive to be "safe" emotional and intellectual territory. Tribes, in this way, function much like cults.

Andrew Sullivan writes that tribalism is attractive because people do not have to think very much; their tribe gives them information that reinforces their personal opinions and discourages them from interacting with others who may hold differing opinions.

Eventually, tribe members are only friends with other tribe members who share and affirm their perspective without contributing to or challenging it. By only interacting with one set of ideas, tribe members lose the ability to relate to members of other tribes; they come to think of anyone who disagrees with them as stupid, backward, or sinister. After a while, members of different tribes have nothing but utter contempt for each other.[11]

In America, tribalism has risen to the point—as mentioned earlier in the civility chapter—where people are dividing themselves geographically. Members of the progressive tribe have enclaved themselves on the coasts and in major urban centers. Members of the conservative tribe continue to move to the South and Southwest. People talk with pride about living in a "blue" (Democrat) state or a "red" (Republican) state. Moreover, even within these partisan tribes there are smaller tribes as small groups within the two major parties bicker with each other about who represents the ideological purity of the party.

How did this radical individualism and subsequent tribalism set in? There are numerous explanations.

As mentioned earlier, the rise of the Internet has made it so that Americans do not have to leave their homes to shop—which used to be a natural opportunity to interact with others—whether it be at the neighborhood grocery store, a bookstore, or another place of commerce. Previous generations went to the grocery store with their parents and observed them stopping to talk with other neighborhood friends as they roamed the aisles buying the week's groceries.

In addition, before they could download books onto their computers, people used to go to libraries, where they ran into friends and neighbors. Before they could stream a sermon over the Internet, people went to church to hear from their pastor and have a chance to connect with others. With corporations offering grocery delivery services and same-day delivery of purchases, there are fewer and fewer reasons for

Americans to leave their homes and fewer opportunities for spontaneous interactions with neighbors.

However, technology-based isolation is only a symptom of a greater problem. Within a healthy society, technology would not necessarily lead to greater isolation; the fact that so many people take refuge in these conveniences to the detriment of social interactions indicates a deeper issue.

Salena Zito, national political reporter for the *Washington Examiner*, offers one explanation for how America has lost its sense of community. She writes that America in its first two hundred years was a nation built on civic groups and other associations, which helped create tight-knit communities. As Tocqueville said, such associations "form a society," and in their absence, society disintegrates into individualism.

Zito points to evidence that Americans are no longer joining these groups. Church attendance continues to decline,[12] and civic group attendance has been declining for more than thirty years.[13] She believes one reason for this is the rise of government; as government grows and takes over more areas of life, it eliminates the need for voluntary associations.

Zito says in the past, voluntary associations played a vital role in communities. Churches fed the poor, brought meals to shut-ins, built hospitals, and performed service projects throughout their community. Civic associations improved schools by providing funds for small, necessary projects. They maintained parks and other nature areas by pulling weeds, planting trees, and raking leaves. Some, like the Lions Clubs, helped fight blindness. Young people, such as the Boy Scouts, engaged in civic projects, helping restore deteriorating neighborhoods and cleaning up cemeteries. She concludes, "[Such associations were] a way to network, and a way to support worthy causes. No politics. No handouts. All from within."[14]

These associations were the "little platoons" that put the needs of the community above the needs of self. Through them, people had ownership of their communities. This ownership meant they had strong civic pride compelling them to work with others to improve the places they lived, from their towns and cities down to their own neighborhoods. But when government—starting with the New Deal and then greatly expanded with the Great Society—started to take over the functions these civic groups used to do, it was a stake to the heart for many of these groups. Many voluntary associations no longer had a reason to exist; if, despite this grim reality, they tried to continue serving in their communities, they faced overwhelming government regulations making it nearly impossible for them. For instance, churches now face stringent zoning codes[15] that often keep them out of neighborhoods, and civic organizations face overreaching health and safety policies that hinder get-togethers like pancake breakfasts, potluck dinners, or athletic competitions.[16]

But even this governmental overreach is only a symptom of the disease. Like technology, a representative government is a tool; its success or failure depends not on it, but on the individuals and communities using it. When we perceive problems with our government, we must look not to the system for a solution. We must look to ourselves.

In his inaugural address, President John F. Kennedy famously quoted Orestes Brownson's statement from 150 years before: "Ask not what your country can do for you, but ask what you can do for your country." [17] While Kennedy, like Daniel Moynihan, was ultimately an advocate of big-government solutions, this statement is the antithesis of the present-day mindset that government will serve as a nanny that takes care of our perceived needs. We have lost a great deal of our community because instead of asking what we can do for others and for our country, we ask others and our country to do things for us.

As with many of the topics we have discussed in this book, people of faith have a particular obligation in this area. Despite the widespread breakdown of church communities that we discussed earlier, churches are still some of the few remaining places where people gather to cultivate genuine relationships. People of faith—people who are connected to a church—have a greater understanding of what true community looks like than many others. This means they have a responsibility to the people in their neighborhoods, their workplaces, and their local areas to model that kind of community and care for others. This takes the form of being intentionally kind and open with our neighbors, seeking them out, building relationships with them, and performing acts of kindness toward them.

While there may be physical fences around our properties, there should be no emotional or relational barriers preventing us from interacting with our neighbors when we see each other in our front yards or getting the mail. Even these small gestures of kindness can go a long way toward restoring a culture of community.

Beyond our neighborhoods—in our churches, our offices, and the places we go for leisure—we must push ourselves outside of our comfort zones. It is far too easy to gravitate toward people of our same age and status in life; true communities are not homogeneous. Instead, a healthy community consists of people from various walks of life, encouraging all its members to practice sympathy toward those who are different from them. This sympathy, however, must be rooted in shared experiences— that is the whole advantage of living in community.

Ben Shapiro writes, "[Restoring community] means we need more communal events—and that means we have to go out of our way to engage with others. We need more shared cultural experiences." [18] Such shared experiences allow us to recognize our differences and move past them into a new, truly diverse kind of unity.

Being part of a community does not mean we all need to agree on everything, but it does mean we all have a vision of working together for the common good. [19] This means putting aside our differences to help our neighbors in times of need and respecting each other's beliefs and opinions to work on solving issues that improve the quality of life in our cities and towns. Just as Patriots and Eagles fans at the Super Bowl could find a way to get along, liberals and conservatives, Christians and non-Christians, and dog lovers and cat lovers should find a way to get along, as well.

But we cannot do these things if we hole up behind closed doors and refuse to know our neighbors or engage with other members of the community. It takes sacrifice—putting the needs of others above our own—if we are going to develop these ties and come back together as a nation.

At the climax of the classic movie *It's a Wonderful Life*, the main character, George Bailey, stands alone on a deserted bridge and contemplates taking his own life. He is saved by Clarence, his guardian angel, who shows him how dramatically different his community would be had he never been part of it. George realizes how much his life has blessed those around him—a realization in itself an immense blessing for him. He realizes, despite the fact that he has not achieved his dreams of travel and wealth, he is truly a rich man because of the relationships composing the fabric of his day-to-day life.

Our riches are not in our individual achievements, our wealth, or our personal experiences and adventures. Our riches are the relationships we have—relationships transcending our personal differences because of our shared striving for the common good. That mindset will help restore community in our nation.

CHAPTER TWELVE

Restoring the Balance between Politics and Culture

"Political problems, even many social problems, are at heart ethical and cultural problems. And improving the attitudes and virtues of a nation is, at best, a slow and halting process." [1]

—Irving Kristol

"Those who based their lives on the unintelligence of sentimentality fight to save themselves with the unintelligence of brutality." [2]

—Richard Weaver, Ideas Have Consequences

I n his book *The Law of Longer Life,* the late British author C. Northcote Parkinson described what he perceived to be the six stages of a culture's descent into decadence and decay. These stages play out over time and come in different orders, but they all lead to the same conclusion.

The first stage, he wrote, is political over-centralization, which leads to the second stage: an inordinate growth in taxation, resulting in government interference in every area of society.

The third stage, necessitated by this government over-involvement, is the growth of a top-heavy system of administration that becomes a giant political machine. To run this machine, the country must enter the fourth stage: the promotion of the wrong people—a.k.a. bureaucrats—to positions of authority.

This leads to the fifth stage: rampant over-spending to feed the needs of the massive bureaucracy, which over time leads to a huge mountain of debt that falls on the shoulders of the society's children and grandchildren. With a national debt of more than twenty-two trillion dollars and growing, American society has reached this point.[3]

Finally, the sixth stage is the encouragement of emotional responses based on sentimentality and the disengagement of critical thinking that weakens the ability of the public to recognize what is amiss, making them willing participants in the cultural decay.[4] We see this in the contradictions of a culture that decries family breakdown while at the same time encouraging the behaviors—such as sex outside of marriage and no-fault divorce—that led to the breakdown in the first place.

America in the twenty-first century is in the throes of all six stages of cultural decay. Although people usually associate dependence on big government and a belief that national problems can be solved by the federal government with the political Left, the reality is that many on the Right take that view, as well. Both sides of the political spectrum have placed their faith in politics to save America, albeit in different ways. The result has been an ongoing societal and cultural slide that neither the Left nor the Right has been successful in arresting, which perhaps is best described in the words of the late jurist Robert Bork: "slouching towards Gomorrah."[5]

We have worked in the highest levels of the federal government and with multiple nationwide Christian ministries and alongside dozens of the leading conservative and Christian leaders of the last four decades. The search by cultural conservatives for a big government solution to internal cultural problems such as family breakdown, disrespect for human life, and other signs of moral decay is something both of us have seen first hand. Between the two of us, we have spent more than fifty years at the intersection of politics and culture seeing many political victories come and go—none of which has ultimately served to halt our nation on the downward slide described by Parkinson.

The great British politician Edmund Burke believed the purpose of politics was not to satisfy the individual wants of the people currently alive, but to maintain and continue a social order that addresses the past, present, and future.[6]

Both of us have found that to be true. From our view on the front lines, we have concluded that politics has definitive limits and we push beyond those limits at our peril. For some conservatives, as with progressive liberals, politics instead of Christ has become their source of salvation, with grave consequences. It has become a way of satisfying individual wants while ignoring the need to maintain the social order that has sustained our nation for the past two hundred-plus years. As a result, America is experiencing both political and cultural chaos.

Instead of dealing with the root causes of America's cultural decay, many seek a political solution that is nothing more than placing a band-aid on a severed artery. As John Stonestreet of the Colson Center writes, "To expect a government or a political party to fix problems that are non-political at root is indeed a form of idolatry."[7]

Looking for peace on earth through politics it is a hollow quest, no matter which side of the political spectrum engages in it. This quest can also be incredibly harmful to the discourse and culture of a nation. When a person or group truly believes their ideas—and *only* their ideas—are capable of creating a paradise on earth, it becomes terribly easy to view people or groups who disagree as enemies of happiness and the human race. If you believe that your political opinions are utterly correct, eminently reasonable, and the only way to prevent totalitarianism it becomes difficult to treat people who disagree with you with respect and dignity. The result is that this quest for paradise through politics leads people and parties to engage in inflammatory rhetoric, and sometimes even in violent actions. Thus, we see the breakdown in civility and goodwill toward others, as discussed earlier.

This happens on both sides of the partisan line. However, in recent years, the progressive Left has begun habitually engaging in this kind of rhetoric, painting its opponents' opinions as idiotic and its opponents themselves as sinister. For the Left, this has led to a terrible self-contradiction because in their quest for political perfection, many progressives have abandoned in practice the principles of tolerance, fairness, and freedom of self-expression they profess to uphold.

Some on the Right, meanwhile, have swallowed the bait and lost sight of the fact that those who oppose their values are human beings with inherent dignity and should be treated with respect, and not scorn. One only needs to read comment sections on the Internet to see conservatives indulging in the same type of venom toward their fellow man that those on the Left use to belittle those who do not agree with them.

During the 2016 presidential election, political rhetoric reached new lows, and the Democratic Party, particularly, had to learn the hard lesson that demonizing those who have legitimate policy disagreements as "bigots" or "extremists" makes more enemies than friends. As we have seen, Democratic nominee Hillary Clinton casually and publicly called everyone who disagreed with her "deplorable." This comment likely contributed to her eventually losing the election.[8] It is also a reflection on how our cultural battles have become so politicized that there is little or no toleration of someone who holds an opposing view.

For conservatives, it is a fundamental premise of political philosophy that politics is a reflection of culture, and not the other way around. As one of our colleagues likes to say, "law follows culture."

In 1991, James Davison Hunter, the LaBrosse-Levinson Distinguished Professor of Religion, Culture, and Social Theory at the University of Virginia and the founder and executive director of UVA's Institute for Advanced Studies in Culture, wrote a book called *Culture Wars: The Struggle to Define America* that succinctly dealt with how culture came to play a pre-eminent role in American politics.

Hunter wrote that for much of American history, the most prominent fault lines were between religious groups, as in the bitter battles over education involving the "Blaine amendments" that arose from Protestant anti-Catholic bigotry and attempted to prohibit government funding of Catholic schools.[9] That started to change as the massive political and cultural upheaval of the 1960s swept across America.

The seeds of these sweeping changes were sown decades before, starting with the so-called Progressive Era right after World War I. For the next several decades, progressives slowly gained control of three of the most important culture-shaping institutions: the nation's public colleges and universities, the entertainment industry, and many churches—especially the historic mainline Protestant denominations.

The seeds planted decades earlier started to bloom in the 1950s, even though that decade is perceived as one of the most politically conservative eras in contemporary American history. The entertainment industry started to push the envelope of what was acceptable more and more. Leftist professors such as Timothy Leary, who openly advocated for illegal drug use, assumed positions of authority at our nation's colleges and universities.[10]

This was all happening while Americans "liked Ike," attended church in record numbers, and moved to comfortable homes in the suburbs. In the meantime, the culture was shifting away from their conservative values, and slowly but surely progressives were completing their long march to reshaping our culture and ultimately our politics, as well.

By the middle of the 1960s, American culture suddenly began changing at breakneck speed. Culture-shapers embraced many things previously seen as morally detrimental to society. For example, *Playboy* magazine was founded in 1953, and by the beginning of the 1960s led to radically new attitudes toward pornography. What was once taboo was seen as an edgy new mode of self-expression.[11]

In 1968, Hollywood tossed aside the production code that had governed the industry for more than three decades. As seen in films such as *Midnight Cowboy*, *A Clockwork Orange*, *The Last Picture Show*, and *The Exorcist*—all of which won or were nominated for Academy Awards—the movie industry embraced a licentious new ethos celebrating graphic portrayals of sex and violence.

On television, family-oriented and non-political comedy shows such as *The Andy Griffith Show*, *Hogan's Heroes*, *Petticoat Junction*, and *The Beverly Hillbillies* were discarded in favor of the coarseness of Norman Lear's *All in the Family* and *Maude*, which promoted the progressive agenda while mocking what had up to that time been mutually-agreed upon values of decency and decorum.

The effect of bringing such things into the mainstream was the rapid coarsening of the culture at large as America started to experience greater disrespect for authority, alarming rises in illicit drug use, crime, and sex outside of marriage, and other social maladies.[12]

In religion, American churches started to question—and, in many cases, ultimately deny—absolute Truth, such as the divinity and resurrection of Christ and the inerrancy of Scripture. As these churches abandoned their theological heritages, many became little more than mouthpieces for progressive political agendas contrary to Scripture and traditional Christianity.[13]

That was the transformation Craig witnessed as a child growing up in Northern California in the late 1960s and early 1970s, when his sleepy little conservative town of Santa Rosa and the Methodist church his family attended became a bastion of far-left liberalism in less than a decade's time.

It did not take long for the law to follow the cultural changes starting to germinate in the 1950s and come into full bloom a decade later. Then came a cascade of Supreme Court decisions: *School District of Abington, Pennsylvania, v. Schempp* in 1963, which abolished school prayer; *Eisenstadt v. Baird* in 1972, which struck down state laws prohibiting the distribution of contraceptives to unmarried persons; and finally, *Roe v. Wade* in 1973, which struck down abortion laws in all fifty states. State legislatures passed many no-fault divorce laws in the late 1960s and 1970s with liberal churches advocating for such laws. By 1977, only 20 percent of American women felt that they should remain in a marriage for the well-being of their children.[14] By the mid-1970s, Christians had become so alarmed at the cultural rot they saw around them that, in a panic, they decided national politics was the solution.

In this decision, unfortunately, many Christians missed a chance to go to the root causes of the problem, which are cultural and individual, not political: the spiritual condition of our friends and neighbors and the resulting breakdown of virtue and culture in our local communities. Just like the Left, which has consistently asserted that bigger government can solve society's ills, conservative Christians embraced the notion that moral government would sweep away the cultural decay.

Interestingly (given today's political dynamics), the first candidate embraced by Christians seeking a political solution was a Democrat: the self-professed "born-again Christian" Jimmy Carter. His public pronouncements of faith inspired millions of religious Americans to give the political system a fresh look, and Carter succeeded in bringing many of them to the ballot box, resulting in his victory over the sitting Republican president, Gerald Ford.

However, the enthusiasm and optimism of religious Americans quickly turned to disappointment and discouragement after Carter became president. His policies turned out to be vastly more liberal than the rhetoric that had inspired Christian conservatives to vote for him in the first place. Particularly disappointing was his inaction on the issue of abortion—an issue that bridged sectarian divides and galvanized conservative evangelicals and conservative Catholics, despite their long-standing theological differences.

This is what James Davison Hunter observed in the 1980s about how the religious and cultural landscape had shifted. After the New York City police broke up a pro-life protest rally including Protestant, Catholic, and Jewish clergy, he observed, "Given the long legacies of anti-Catholicism, and the long legacies of anti-Semitism in America, the fact that you have leaders in these traditions standing arm-in-arm, in protests, was a pretty remarkable thing to see." [15]

Thus, four years later, religious Americans turned on the Carter administration with vengeance. They pinned their hopes on another, very different kind of politician: former California Governor Ronald Reagan, who famously told an audience of conservative Christian leaders in Dallas that while they could not endorse him (because of their tax-exempt status), he endorsed them and what they stood for.[16]

Reagan tapped into the deeply disheartened conservative Evangelical and Catholic base and welcomed them into the Republican fold. This new alliance between conservative American religious groups and the Republican Party fundamentally changed the political landscape, proving to be a reliable base for four successful Republican presidential runs: Reagan, George H. W. Bush, George W. Bush, and Donald Trump. These traditional-values voters became the mainstay of the GOP.

Meanwhile, the Democratic Party continued to drift left, hardening its support for abortion and embracing other progressive agendas. Voters with traditional values, even if they did not wholeheartedly endorse the Republican Party's platform, soon found the Democratic Party was not a viable alternative for them—and indeed, as pro-life Democrats continue to find, they are not welcome there.[17]

Despite these political triumphs for Christian voters in the late twentieth and early twenty-first centuries, we find ourselves today with a culture in an even more advanced state of decay than in the 1970s. The Reagan presidency, in particular, demonstrated to those who were able to see it that political power alone cannot restore virtue to a society.

Even with the most prominent conservative president of the contemporary era in power exerting his best efforts to satisfy his Moral Majority base and promote traditional values, it became clear that politics has its limitations in impacting culture. Throughout Reagan's presidency, Hollywood kept cranking out highly sexualized and violent movies, academia continued its drift away from traditional concepts of morality and reality, and more and more mainline denominations forsook biblical truth in favor of theological relativity. The policy direction from the White House changed, but the direction of the culture did not.

Why? Because the patient was already sick and the cure was not going to come from the federal government. While the Reagan era brought some comfort to religious Americans, ultimately it was just an anesthetic dulling the pain for a while. The cultural cancer continued to spread relatively unabated because the real issue—America's spiritual condition—went untreated.

Rod Dreher, the author of the much-debated Benedict Option we discussed earlier, agrees with this assessment. He said:

> I consider myself a member of the Religious Right insofar as I am a religious and political conservative. But when I think of the religious right, I think of pastors and activists who got congregations wound up to be values voters and to get out there and pull the lever for Republican candidates— if we just capture politics, if we capture the courts, we'll capture culture.

He goes on to say, while the church was preaching political involvement, the cultural Left was capturing the imaginations of our children and the American people, and the only answer the church had was politics. He states, since politics reflects culture, by focusing on politics instead of culture, we now have an even worse predicament.[18]

Russell Kirk, the great conservative philosopher, put the problem best when he wrote that social and cultural crises are ultimately spiritual and moral crises. "Political problems, at bottom, are religious and moral problems." He said if a nation wanted to maintain order within its boundaries, it would first have to attain order in the souls of its citizens. This order cannot be created or enforced by merely political means.

Kirk's words could not have been more correct. The underlying problem is that all of us have holes in our souls, and countless individuals on the Left and the Right alike are looking to fill that empty vacuum with everything but God. Politics, for many, is simply another attempt to fill the emptiness only Christ can fill. As people elevate politics to the level of God, they become excessively invested in political outcomes and they escalate political conflicts to a disproportionate level with grievous cultural consequences.

Jonah Goldberg, who is Jewish, explains the problem this way, writing, "Partisans are convinced that the answers to their woes lies in total victory over the other. This is disastrous, because the embrace of partisan identity exacerbates the problem, and because our government was never meant to fill the holes in their souls." [19]

Too many on both the Left and on the Right presume that the most pressing problems of our time can be solved in the political boxing ring by pummeling our opponents into bloody submission. The result, as we have discussed previously, is the collapse of civility and a spike in vitriol among people who disagree, as well as political gridlock stemming from the perceived impossibility of compromises. This means that none of our nation's problems are solved. On both sides, people reason this way: "If we can just get the right political calculus into place; if we could just elect the right men and women to office; we could begin the vital work of righting the proverbial ship of state and the fate of our country." There is no room here for compromise or civility.

This is a miscalculation of the first order. If Americans continue to place their faith in what the political class can do for society, they will continue to be disappointed. Such a misguided faith in a political savior, so to speak, can never fully deliver because politics cannot adequately address or resolve the most pressing moral and cultural concerns facing us. Government cannot solve the problems we have discussed. In fact, it has demonstrated time and again it can only make them worse.

We are not suggesting politics is unimportant—quite the opposite. Many of America's current problems are the result of Christians' apathy toward the political process during the 1950s and 1960s, which allowed progressives to mobilize actively and capture the key institutions of education, media and entertainment, and mainstream religion.

As Christians, we are called to be "salt and light" in our culture and to stand for justice and righteousness. One highly significant way in which we can live out those callings is by being involved in government on every level. We know from Scripture and from history that what happens in the halls of power matters, and Christians are honor-bound to be fully engaged in that space, seeking to bring about the virtuous ends of God-ordained government.

John Stonestreet says Christians must keep in mind that politics will either contribute to or counter what he calls our "cultural confusions." He is clear about the ramifications of this for Christians: "So politics matters. Still. A lot. We must stay engaged."[20] But to use his term, the underlying problem is not political confusion; it is cultural confusion, and culture is shaped not in Washington, D.C., but in towns and communities across America.

Former Speaker of the House Tip O'Neill famously said, "All politics is local." There is a profound truth in that statement. While both state and national politics are useful and central to the American way of life, it ultimately is at a local level where we must work to restore our culture. It was at this same local level that far-left activists launched their efforts to change radically the views of ordinary Americans. Their "little platoons" slowly took over the local institutions—the colleges and universities, the churches, the movie theatres, the living rooms via television, and the halls of city and county governments. They were passionate about what they believed to be true, and even though their views did not represent those of most Americans, their incessant drive eventually allowed them to achieve their goals and move the needle within mainstream culture.

It is critical that Christians be engaged in both culture and politics, but if we only engage at a superficial level in either, we are doomed to failure. Like so many other worthy endeavors, it will take perseverance to reverse America's cultural decay, and there will be times where it seems impossible. And our efforts must start at the most basic grass-roots: in our homes and communities.

The way to begin is for individual Christians to become more involved than ever in the civic life of our nation in those little platoons—the mediating structures of neighborhoods, families, churches, and voluntary associations. These mediating structures are where our current cultural decay took root as neighborhoods fragmented, families disintegrated, churches forsook truth, and colleges and universities abandoned their original purpose of higher education and became political weapons for the Left.

Thus, withdrawing from politics and the greater culture is not an option. On the cultural level, involvement can take several different forms including simply running for office. For some, it could mean going to the places most directly dealing with shattered and broken lives. Those include crisis pregnancy centers; shelters for battered women and victims of sex trafficking; working with children, youth, and young adults; and so forth. For others, it could mean getting involved in areas directly affecting future generations, whether it be school boards, PTAs, youth groups, or mentoring young couples.

The bottom line is this: we are not all called to be political activists, but we *are* all called to be "salt and light" in our spheres of influence, no matter the sphere. The only way to bring about a renewal of our culture is to maintain the proper balance between the two spheres of politics and culture; we must be active in forming strong, healthy "little platoons" in our communities while being active participants in the civic discourse.

That is the proper balance between politics and culture and that is how America's current political and cultural chaos can be quelled and social order can be restored for future generations.

CHAPTER THIRTEEN

Restoring the Constitution

"While often overlooked, and likely taken for granted, the Constitution is central to American life.... It orders our politics, defines our nation, and protects our citizens as a free people." [1]

—Matthew Spalding, director of the B. Kenneth Simon Center for American Studies at the Heritage Foundation

"We are under a Constitution, but the Constitution is what the judges say it is." [2]

—Supreme Court Chief Justice Charles Evans Hughes

"The accumulation of all powers, legislative, executive, and judiciary, in the same hands, whether of one, a few, or many, and whether hereditary, self-appointed, or elective, may justly be pronounced the very definition of tyranny." [3]

—James Madison, *The Federalist* No. 47

"'We the people'" adopted a written Constitution precisely because it has a fixed meaning, a meaning that does not change." [4]

—Associate Supreme Court Justice Clarence Thomas

S everal years ago, a group of leading progressive jurists produced a document titled, "The Constitution in 2020." The document laid out their vision of how a progressive constitutional interpretation would transform the way the Constitution is applied to American law. This interpretation would accommodate new "constitutional rights" to guaranteed income, government-funded childcare, increased access to abortion and physician-assisted suicide, liberalization of drug abuse laws, and open borders.[5]

These activists represent the extreme end of one school of thought within constitutional interpretation—the school known as "living constitutionalism." Living constitutionalists believe the meaning of the Constitution is fluid and the task of the interpreter is to apply that meaning to specific situations to accommodate cultural changes. In other words, living constitutionalists believe the language—and therefore, the principles that language represents—of the Constitution must be interpreted in light of culture.

Former President Woodrow Wilson, one of the earliest advocates of living constitutionalism, summarized this view this way:

> Society is a living organism and must obey the laws of life, not of mechanics; it must develop. All progressives ask or desire is permission—in an era when "development," "evolution," is the scientific word—to interpret the Constitution according to the Darwinian principle; all they ask is recognition of the fact that a nation is a living thing and not a machine.[6]

What Wilson was saying, in a somewhat convoluted academic manner, was the Constitution was meant to "evolve" past its original state and, in his view and the view of other progressives, should not be seen as a stagnant document. However, one of the reasons Wilson and the progressives felt this way was because the Constitution, as written, did not allow for the advancement of their particular worldview.

Ronald J. Pestritto, graduate dean and professor of politics at Hillsdale College, writes that Wilson was a vocal critic of the Founding Fathers. Wilson, he says, saw the system of separation of powers outlined in the Constitution as a barrier to progressivism. To overcome this barrier, Wilson and other progressives developed a flexible approach to interpreting the Constitution—one permitting them to sidestep the parts of the Constitution standing in their way. Pestritto writes, "Wilson understood that the limits placed upon the power of the national government by the Constitution—limits that Progressives wanted to see relaxed if not removed—were grounded in the natural-rights principles of the Declaration of Independence."[7]

Under a "living Constitution" approach, the meaning of the Constitution can be stretched far beyond the intentions of the Founding Fathers. One of the best-known examples of this came from Justice William O. Douglas's opinion in the case *Griswold v. Connecticut* where he wrote, through examining "emanations from penumbras," he discerned a "right to privacy" in the Fourteenth Amendment that allowed the Court to overturn laws prohibiting contraception. Douglas's opinion served as the legal precedent for *Roe v. Wade.*[8]

Another example came in the 1992 decision in *Planned Parenthood v. Casey,* when Justice Anthony Kennedy, along with Justices Sandra Day O'Connor and David Souter (all Republican appointees), concocted seemingly out of thin air a so-called right to define one's own liberty and existence to uphold *Roe v. Wade.* Kennedy wrote in the plurality opinion:

> These matters [abortion], involving the most intimate and personal choices a person may make in a lifetime, choices central to personal dignity and autonomy, are central to the liberty protected by the Fourteenth Amendment. At the heart of liberty is the right to define one's own concept of existence, of meaning, of the universe, and of the mystery of human life.[9]

This is "living constitutionalism" at its zenith, where man can now determine what is right and wrong in his own eyes, rather than by the fundamental God-given rights upon which our Constitution was based.

On the other end of the spectrum is the school of thought known as "originalism." Though originalism has existed as long as justices have sought to interpret the Constitution, over the past few decades it has garnered far more attention than in the past. This is partly because of the outspokenness of contemporary living constitutionalism, which necessarily throws originalism into sharp relief. In addition, originalism has had some very high-profile advocates in the recent past, most notably the former Attorney General Edwin Meese III[10] and the late Associate Justice Antonin Scalia.[11]

Originalism is an attempt to understand and apply the words of the Constitution as they were intended, working only within the limits of what the Founding Fathers could have meant when they drafted the text in 1787. This interpretative method requires judges to consider the ideas and intellects that influenced the Founders, most notably British enlightenment thinkers like John Locke and Edmund Burke, as well as the Christian Scriptures.

The Founders left plenty of content outlining their own perspectives that yields insight into how they thought about the Constitution. Speaking to the Massachusetts Militia, John Adams said the vision presented in the Constitution was achievable only by "a moral and religious people." He added, "It is wholly inadequate to the government of any other."[12] For the originalist, these words are not mere throwaways; they are intrinsic to interpreting the Constitution and understanding how the American government is to function. As a result, it is necessary to look at the historical context for insight into the way Adams understood those words.

Morality, both for the individual and for the state, was a powerful, motivating force for Enlightenment thinkers from Immanuel Kant to John Locke and went hand in hand with the concept of liberty. Without morality, there can be no liberty. Moreover, the idea from the Christian tradition of "a righteous people" elevates our vision beyond mere civil order to a transcendent order, an order rooted in a right relationship between God and man. For the originalist, these concepts must be guiding influences on interpreting the Constitution for the simple reason that they were guiding influences on writing the Constitution.

The "living Constitution" philosophy, on the other hand, presents a direct threat to the three-pronged system of government established by the Founders—a system designed to create checks and balances and to prevent power from being concentrated in the hands of one person or small group of people. The threat comes from living constitutionalism's excessive trust in the judiciary.

The task of the judicial branch, whose highest representatives are the justices of the Supreme Court, is to interpret the Constitution and consider existing laws in its light. In the 1803 case of *Marbury v. Madison*, Chief Justice John Marshall wrote that the Court could review decisions made by the legislative and executive branches and declare them unconstitutional.[13] The case involved a last-minute political commission by President John Adams to William Marbury subsequently denied by Adams's successor, Thomas Jefferson. Without going into the details of the case, this decision resulted in the judicial branch asserting constitutional authority over the other two branches of government, which had not previously been the case.

Since then, that authority has grown to the point where the judiciary not only reviews law, but actively participates in making law—the essence of living constitutionalism. More than once, living constitutionalism has led to the Supreme Court dictating what the law of the land ought to be, essentially stripping the legislature of its designated powers. That is what happened in *Roe v. Wade* (creating a right to abortion).

As living constitutionalist justices "discover" rights not stated clearly in the Constitution, they wield the judicial system like a weapon and take a disproportionate role in shaping the laws. For example, in 1973 when *Roe v. Wade* was decided, forty-six states had laws restricting abortion. Only four had fully legalized it.[14] The Supreme Court's decision—based not on language found in the Constitution, but on extrapolations from a particular contemporary interpretation of the Fourteenth Amendment—overturned those forty-six state laws, effectively stripping the state legislatures of their power and communicating to the citizens that their opinion on abortion did not matter—despite the total lack of language pertaining to abortion in the Constitution.

Defenders of living constitutionalism claim it gives greater flexibility to the law because it allows judges to interpret laws in light of contemporary values, rather than requiring them to understand and apply timeless principles to situations unthinkable to the Founding Fathers. In contrast, originalists believe living constitutionalism presents a threat to social stability because the continual discovery of new rights protected by a so-called living Constitution necessarily leads to legal irregularity. Under living constitutionalism, law becomes governed not by principles, but by fads, and what is legally and morally justified shifts from day to day according to what is fashionable. Living constitutionalism undermines the rule of law and disrupts the process for how laws are created, which in a constitutional republic is by state and federal legislators who are elected by the people.

In response to this, Justice Antonin Scalia warned in a 2005 speech that it is the opposite; rather than safeguarding the rights of citizens against a rigid judiciary, living constitutionalism strips the democratic system of any flexibility it might have by giving an unelected judiciary the ability to impose laws without being held accountable by voters. He said, "If you think aficionados of a living Constitution want to bring you flexibility, think again." He added, "The problem with the living

Constitution in a word is that somebody needs to decide how it grows." That someone is generally not the average voting citizen.

Scalia went on to defend the Constitution's division of powers that grants citizens and state legislatures, not the courts, the right to make laws. "You think the death penalty is a good idea? Persuade your citizens to adopt it. You want a right to abortion? Persuade your fellow citizens to enact it? That's flexibility." [15] What he is saying is that under the Constitution, it is the legislature's prescribed role to make the laws—not the courts. When the court supersedes the legislative process and makes laws with popular consensus behind it, the people feel, rightfully so, that their voice on important issues is being ignored.

As Adam J. White wrote in a tribute to Justice Scalia after his passing in 2016, "[Scalia] stressed that the proper role of judges in our constitutional system is crucial but limited: courts should interpret the meaning of laws but the vast bulk of governance should be left to the people's representatives." [16]

Writing in *National Review*, Victor David Hanson of the Hoover Institution expounded on the ways progressive judicial activists twist the Constitution and delved into the difference between how progressives and conservatives view the role of the courts. Hanson explains how progressive activists see the courts as a political institution, while conservatives view the courts as guardians of the original intent of the Constitution. That is why when progressives cannot achieve their goals politically through legislatures or a vote of the people, they go to the courts to achieve their political aims. This view was summarized by Roger Baldwin, the founder of the ACLU, who once said, "I placed my faith in the courts" [17] to achieve his progressive objectives.

In Hanson's words, progressives believe a highly educated elite should "by fiat override both presidential executive orders and congressional and state legislation in order to accomplish what they perceive to be 'good' for Americans."

Hanson wrote, "They do this even if the people do not want the change, or in the progressive's view, are incapable of appreciating the 'good' that has just been accomplished, in the view of those who advocate for a 'living Constitution.'" [18]

The current battle over Supreme Court judicial nominations comes down to these two competing judicial philosophies—originalism versus living constitutionalism. Living constitutionalists, who seemed unstoppable in the 1960s and 1970s, met stiff resistance from the Reagan administration, which reprioritized originalism.

Through the arguments put forth by Attorney General Meese and Justice Scalia, originalism has become a thriving alternative interpretive method with many prominent adherents. The progressive effort to use the courts to reshape the Constitution has slowed, but the battles over the courts have heated up. Progressives, used to decades of victories, now face a robust, articulate group of originalists who are equally dedicated to advocating for their interpretive method. Recognizing this, living constitutionalists fear if a majority of the Supreme Court justices are originalists, many of their previous victories, such as *Roe v. Wade*, could be limited or even overturned.

Today, progressives resist the confirmation of originalist judges at the federal appellate and Supreme Court levels with some of the most violently inflamed rhetoric of American politics. Whenever a justice is nominated to serve on the court by a conservative president, progressives engage in a "Stop (fill in the name)" campaign, warning that any presidential nominee will take the nation, in their view, "back to the dark ages." For example, when President Trump nominated Judge Brett Kavanaugh for the bench to replace retiring Justice Anthony Kennedy, protestors already had signs made up declaring "Stop (fill in the name)" for all four of the perceived finalists for the nomination.

The escalating conflict between originalism and living constitutionalism is symptomatic of America's increasing polarization. Even though it may seem a bit esoteric, it is vital that ordinary Americans—even those who have never attended a constitutional law class or who have no desire to go to law school—seek to understand this conflict and develop an informed perspective. For those of us who incline toward an originalist perspective, a good place to begin understanding the nuances of this debate is the life and writing of Justice Scalia.

Justice Scalia modeled a unique and compelling way to engage in this often hostile debate. He defended originalism forcefully and eloquently, never backing down from his belief that laws ought to be made by elected legislators, not judges. But even more noteworthy than his staunch philosophical convictions is the way he engaged with his ideological opponents. Scalia maintained decades-long friendships with stalwart living constitutionalists who vehemently disagreed with his interpretive methods. After his death, two of the most committed living constitutionalists on the Supreme Court—Justices Ruth Bader Ginsburg and Elena Kagan—delivered tributes to Scalia praising his grace and personal warmth.

Justice Kagan said, "His views of interpreting texts have changed the way all of us think and talk about the law. I admired Nino [his nickname] for his brilliance and erudition, his dedication and energy, and his peerless writing. And I treasured Nino's friendship. I will always remember, and greatly miss, his warmth, charm, and generosity." [19]

In our "little platoons," we can imitate Justice Scalia by standing strong for our principles while showing charity and true friendship toward those who do not share them. We can encourage each other to be involved citizens. It is vital we know our history and the basics of our Constitution, as this will help us not be swayed by arguments that undermine the foundational principles of our government.

Earlier, we mentioned the statement, "Law follows culture." We would like to add an addendum to that statement: "Law enables culture." What goes on in the culture greatly influences the law, like progressive judicial activists who seek to implement their cultural views via American jurisprudence. However, the law can also slow the advancement of pernicious social trends and restore constitutional order if it is in the hands of those who adhere to an originalist view of the Constitution.

In a speech given just weeks before his death, Justice Scalia expressed his belief that America is a religious republic and faith is a central part of our national life and constitutional understanding. He went on to say the Lord has been generous to the United States because Americans honored God,[20] even though, as human beings, we have been far from perfect. In his view, if renewal was to occur, the original intent of the Constitution must be restored to outline a form of government built on respect for human dignity, which brings with it respect for true freedom.

It is that understanding that will help restore our government to the intentions of the Founding Fathers—a government by the people, of the people, and for the people.

CHAPTER FOURTEEN

Restoring Patriotism and Sacrifice

*"Patriotism means love of country (patria, in the Latin) and implies
a readiness to sacrifice for it, to fight for it, perhaps even to give one's
life for it."* [1]

**— Walter Berns, American Enterprise Institute, professor emeritus at
Georgetown University**

*"Oh, say does that star-spangled banner yet wave
O'er the land of the free and the home of the brave?"*

— "The Star-Spangled Banner"

*"I pledge allegiance to the flag of the United States of America, and to
the republic for which it stands, one nation under God, indivisible, with
liberty and justice for all."*

— "The Pledge of Allegiance"

*"God bless America, land that I love.
Stand beside her and guide her,
Through the night with the light from above."*

— "God Bless America" by Irving Berlin

Irving Berlin was born Israel Baline on May 11, 1888, in Temun,
Siberia. When he was very young, his Russian-Jewish parents fled
to America to escape religious persecution. The young boy grew
up with a deep appreciation for the freedom he and his family experienced in their new home, where their lives were no longer in danger

simply because of what they believed, and there was equality of opportunity for a young man to succeed in life.

This young Russian immigrant went on to write music that defined what it meant to be an American patriot for much of the twentieth century. His tunes offered hope and inspiration during the bleak times of World War I, the Great Depression, and World War II. His lyrics rejoiced in the blessings he had received through the American way of life. His songs—including "White Christmas" and "Easter Parade"— were celebrations of American traditions and culture.[2]

However, of all his works, "God Bless America" continues to have the strongest impact on the American psyche. While it had been a staple for a long time, this was never more evident than in the days after the terrorist attacks of September 11, 2001. Despite the increasing secularization and division of American culture, "God Bless America" was sung in the halls of Congress, in sports stadiums, and other venues as a sort of alternative national anthem that expressed patriotic hope in the wake of tragedy.

In a 2014 interview, Berlin's daughter, Mary Ellin Barrett, said, "I understood that that song was his 'thank you' to the country that had taken him in. It was the song of the immigrant boy who made good."[3]

Some have misconstrued "God Bless America" as a song that implies that God only blesses America and that our nation has a spiritual superiority over other nations. That was not the intention of Irving Berlin. He meant it as a way of saying thank you to a nation that had given him freedom and opportunity that cannot be found anywhere else on earth. Berlin was a patriot—someone who understood how special America was and how blessed he was to live there. Because he recognized how he had been blessed, he could not help but be thankful.

The statue of another, less well-known American patriot stands in Washington's National Cathedral: Norman Prince, who was among the one hundred thousand Americans who lost their lives in World War I. In a city adorned with ornate statues and buildings, his statue is simple and singular. It stands in a quiet corner of the cathedral as a silent witness to the patriotism and self-sacrifice that defined one of America's deadliest wars.

Today, Norman Prince is largely forgotten. Only a few of the many visitors to the National Cathedral know who the young war hero was or what he did. Prince was one of the founders of the Lafayette Escadrille, the most famous squadron of American flyers in France. The pilots of the Escadrille also served as the pioneering squadron of what would eventually become the United States Army Air Corps, the modern-day Air Force.

Prince was a native New Englander and a graduate of Harvard Law School. Despite the fact that he had an impressive career in front of him, he knew that one of America's greatest allies—France, who had supported America in our fight for freedom—was under siege. He felt called to make a personal sacrifice to protect their freedom. Since the airplane was still a new invention and the United States did not have an army air corps, he volunteered with other young Americans to form a squadron to defend France against Kaiser Wilhelm's air force—the most deadly in the world at the time.

Even before America formally joined the war effort in 1917, the members of the Escadrille felt it was their solemn duty as American citizens to defend freedom where it was most hotly under assault. It was a decision not made lightly; the planes used in World War I were infamously dangerous and unreliable, and parachutes were still a thing of the future. Each of the members of the Escadrille chose to join with the knowledge that he likely was going to his death.

"They all led comfortable lives, at least most of them did," says Paul Glenshaw, a filmmaker in Silver Spring, Maryland, who is making a documentary film about the Escadrille. "They had no business being there ... many of them knowing that they would not survive." [4] Of the original thrity-eight members who made up the squadron, ten lost their lives—including Prince.

Before he died, Prince took a much-deserved leave from the war and took the opportunity to tell a Boston audience what it was like to serve in a massive global conflict, saying, "The terrible racket and spectacle of shells exploding nearby made me shiver. My limbs began to tremble.... My legs went so wobbly... that I tried to hide them from my observer, who was an old hand at the game. I confess to the feeling of relief when we reached the point where our bombs were to be thrown over." [5]

In 1916, just a few months after he spoke in Boston, Prince was killed when his airplane crashed and he was thrown out, breaking both his legs and fracturing his skull. For three days, he was in a coma, and he eventually succumbed to his injuries. In those three days, the French government bestowed upon him one of its highest medals for valor: the French Legion of Honor. And during his funeral in France, planes dropped flowers from the sky to honor him and his service. For the next twenty years, his body laid in state at the Lafayette Escadrille Memorial near Paris.

In 1937, his parents commissioned the construction of a small chapel inside the Washington National Cathedral in honor of their son. They removed his remains from France and brought him home to rest on the American soil he loved so deeply. Prince's body traveled from France to Washington, D.C., in a flag-draped coffin. On the final leg of the journey—from Union Station to the cathedral—U.S. Army airplanes flew in tribute overhead.

At about the same time, Irving Berlin, who had written "God Bless America" during the height of World War I, was re-writing his lyrics as another threat to freedom loomed over the world—the Axis Powers—with an updated version emerging in late 1938. Berlin felt that the song should be one that embraced peace and unity in the wake of the Axis threat. He removed lyrics that might be misconstrued as taking a political stance (such as removing the words "to the right" and replacing them with "through the night"). He also added an intro that is rarely heard today that said, "While the storm clouds gather far across the sea / Let us swear allegiance to a land that's free / Let us all be grateful for a land so fair, / As we raise our voices in a solemn prayer."[6]

No one should confuse the love of country with the gospel of Jesus Christ. As stated earlier, Berlin was Jewish and he just wanted to express his gratefulness to God for the blessings he had received in his new land. Norman Prince's sacrificial service to help his brothers and sisters in France demonstrates how good citizenship and patriotism often flow from faith in God and gratitude to Him.

Unfortunately, in recent years, this type of patriotism has come under increasing attack. In the first chapter of the book, we discussed how the teaching of American history had changed from showing gratitude for our freedoms to promoting a succession of grievances against the country. Thus, Americans are pitted against each other rather than brought together in unity—despite our personal political and religious views. The motives of those, such as Irving Berlin, who loved the opportunity and freedoms he found in his adopted land are questioned. The heroism and sacrifice of men like Norman Prince and the Escadrille are dismissed and forgotten.

No, we are not perfect. Yes, there is injustice in society and it needs to be rooted out and dealt with. Yes, we still suffer from the sin of racism that has plagued our nation since before its founding era. On that, there is no argument. But no other nation on earth, despite its ills, has given its people more for which to be grateful. Unlike other nations, we have freedom of religion, freedom of speech, freedom to peacefully assemble—to name just a few of the freedoms that people in other nations do not have.

That is why we need to put our differences aside and realize that regardless of our race, religion, political beliefs, or whatever disagreements we may have, ultimately we are all made in the image of God and are one, united together—E Pluribus Unum—for the greater good of all. We must empathize with each other, rather than attack each other, if we are going to be one nation indivisible.

When America came together to help the devastated families of Hurricane Harvey in 2017, writer Peggy Noonan observed, "My beloved America, you're not a mirage. You're still here."[7] What we witnessed in the aftermath of the hurricane was true patriotism. Being a patriot means sacrificing for others, like the furniture store owners who allowed people fleeing the floods to sleep in the clean beds they were planning to sell. Sacrifice also means meeting someone with whom you disagree, getting to know him or her, and thoughtfully listening to his or her perspective. Most of all, we are motivated by our gratitude to God—and because each person is made in his image—to love and sacrifice for our fellow citizens with whom we live side by side in freedom.

It is because of this love and gratitude for God, our country, and each other that individuals such as Norman Prince laid down their lives for people they may never have met, but to whom they were bound as fellow lovers of freedom. It is why we put aside our differences and help those devastated by Hurricane Harvey, a horrible earthquake, or some other sort of disaster. It is why in the days after the horrific attacks of 9/11, Americans of all stripes gathered together and sang "God Bless America," because like Irving Berlin and Norman Prince, we know, deep in our hearts, that we have been blessed by God—even if we do not deserve it—with the precious gift of freedom.

CHAPTER FIFTEEN

Restoring America

"We, and most of the people in the World, still believe in a civilization of construction and not of destruction. We, and most of the people in the world, still believe that men and women have an inherent right to hew out the patterns of their own individual lives, just so long as they as individuals do not harm their fellow beings. We call this ideal, by many terms which are synonymous—we call it individual liberty, we call it civil liberty and, I think, best of all, we call it democracy." [1]

—President Franklin Delano Roosevelt

"Only our deep moral values and our strong social institutions can hold back that jungle and restrain the darker impulses of human nature." [2]

—President Ronald Reagan

"However, in early democracies, as in the American democracy at the time of its birth, all individual human rights were granted because man is God's creature. That is, freedom was given to the individual conditionally, in the assumption of his constant religious responsibility. Such was the heritage of the preceding thousand years. Two hundred or even fifty years ago, it would have seemed quite impossible, in America, that an individual could be granted boundless freedom simply for the satisfaction of his instincts or whims. Subsequently, however, all such limitations were discarded everywhere in the West; a total liberation occurred from the moral heritage of Christian centuries with their great reserves of mercy and sacrifice. State systems were—State systems were becoming increasingly and totally materialistic. The West ended up by truly enforcing human rights, sometimes even excessively, but man's sense of responsibility to God and society grew dimmer and dimmer." [3]

—Aleksandr Solzhenitsyn, Harvard University, 1978

"The Church cannot be, in any political sense, either conservative, liberal, or revolutionary. Conservativism is too often conservation of the wrong things: liberalism is a relaxation of discipline; revolution a denial of the permanent things." [4]

—**T. S. Eliot**

A s we survey American history, it becomes evident that our country has experienced two revolutions. Each had a profound impact on our country—one for good and one for ill.

The first revolution—the American Revolution—resulted in an upward trajectory for the United States of America as the new nation was guided by the rule of law and fostered strong, enduring families and communities in both urban and rural settings.

America's Founders, while not all religious men, understood that for the new nation to survive and thrive, it had to be built on a shared belief in a transcendent order.

It was this belief in transcendent order—despite whatever political, cultural, or economic differences we had—that united Americans for the most part for nearly two centuries. Unfortunately, as individuals are prone to do because of their sinful nature, Americans—while openly professing belief in God—compromised this transcendent order through their toleration of the sins of slavery and racism. The result was the horrific physical and societal carnage of the Civil War and so many other societal ills afterward. These divisions still plague us today as we still live in a country divided against itself, instead of unified in purpose.

Despite this egregious error in judgment that unfortunately cannot be reversed, American families, for the most part, were intact, healthy civic pride abounded, education flourished, and equality of opportunity was available for those who pursued it—regardless of the obstacles put up by their fellow man.

But in the 1960s, America experienced a second revolution: the Sexual Revolution. It was during this period that the American family, which served as the backbone of society, was dismissed as "outmoded" and "patriarchal." Abortion, while always sadly present in our society, went from something seen as a tragedy to something to be celebrated. Sexual relations outside of marriage were trumpeted as the new norm and virginity became mocked. We forsook the virtues that stabilized our nation for generations, despite the tolerance of other sins, such as slavery and racism.

Our Founders rightly warned that we could not have freedom without virtue. But since the 1960s, a large portion of our nation has chosen to forsake virtue for license. The result has been the loss of freedom—whether it be religious freedom, free speech, or freedom of association—an ever-expanding government, out-of-control federal spending, a dysfunctional educational system resulting in diminished economic opportunities, incivility, and the breakdown of the family.

If America's restoration is to occur, it will need to undergo a third revolution—one that returns it to the spiritual foundation upon which it was built. America will not resolve its current crisis without a restoration of faith.

That is why the ongoing attacks on our faith and values we have discussed throughout this book are so pernicious and must be addressed. The English philosopher Roger Scruton has observed that besides its external enemies, the West confronts "a militant atheism at home," which is among the greatest threats to our way of life.[5] This militant atheism, or secularism, in which one lives for self-fulfillment rather than for a higher purpose changes our perspective from "one for all" to "every man for himself." When the self is elevated over a higher purpose, society begins to collapse from the inside. That elevation of self was at the core of the Sexual Revolution, and today we are on the edge of complete societal collapse.

Despite all this, we are confident an American restoration lies in our future if we have the courage and conviction to strive for it. Jewish historian Gertrude Himmelfarb writes how through the "remoralizing" of our most important institutions and assumptions we can restore our society on a spiritual and cultural level. Like many others, Himmelfarb draws a direct line from a strong civil society—made up of institutions like family, community, church, and private enterprise—to a strong nation. People learn to function as "free, responsible, moral adults" in these institutions and apply that responsibility and morality as citizens of a nation.

In light of the Sexual Revolution, however, Himmelfarb wrote that we must divest ourselves of unrealistic expectations because some institutions may be beyond repair. She wrote:

> Some families are too dysfunctional to perform the roles assigned to them; if not actually dysfunctional, then so weakened by divorce, serial cohabitation, and single parenthood as to be of little avail in the task ahead. So too, private and communal associations, even many churches, are so permeated by the dominant cultural values that they can hardly serve as paragons of morality and responsibility. It is evidently not enough to revitalize civil society; we have the far more difficult task of remoralizing it.[6]

After reading Himmelfarb's quote, one is prone to ask the question, "So, what's the use?" Does she mean families are so far gone they are beyond repair, and our houses of worship can no longer be light in an increasingly darkened culture? Does she mean we just need to withdraw from every institution and let our entire society collapse under its own decaying weight, so it can then be "remoralized?"

That is not what Himmelfarb is saying. What she is saying is we cannot just pine for the bygone days before the Sexual Revolution and have an unrealistic expectation that we can eventually return to a society modeling the virtues of that era. Particularly in the case of the family, the Sexual Revolution has done too much damage for some families to ever be restored. While certain resilient individuals can break the cycle of generational family dysfunction, they tend to be the exception, and not the rule. She is also saying it is going to take more than restoring a civil society to bring about American renewal. If that were the case, it would be a fairly easy cure. Instead, it is going to take a deliberate effort to re-establish the values as enumerated in the Declaration of Independence: life, liberty, and the pursuit of happiness.

While we may not be able to return America to days gone by, we can still impact the current cultural climate to slow and hopefully bring a halt to further decay. To accomplish this, we need to focus on restoring what Edmund Burke and T. S. Eliot, among others, called the "permanent things." The great conservative Russell Kirk defined these "permanent things" as "a patrimony of order, justice, and freedom, a tolerable moral order, and an inheritance of culture"[7] based on ideals of Western civilization that recognize all rights come directly from our Creator, and not from man.

In order to restore these "permanent things" in our nation, Kirk says we must first educate the public on the dangers of the ideas being promoted by the progressive movement. According to Kirk, those ideas include the militant secularism that places man at the center of existence; arrogant relativism, which argues there is no absolute truth and all points of view are equally valid; and soft socialism, which approves of government regulation of our lives in every economic and social area.[8]

In *The Conservative Mind*, Kirk writes about how we can counter these damaging ideas. Instead of secularism, he says, the conservative looks to a transcendent ontological and moral order that regulates society and informs personal conscience. Instead of relativism, the conservative points to the eternal truths found in Scripture that guide human behavior and affirm all individuals have inherent worth and dignity. Instead of socialism, the conservative declares freedom and private property are inextricably linked.

The vision of conservatives is not of a utopia without faults—because all of history tells us that this is impossible. Instead, conservatives aspire to a functioning society that can deal honestly and justly with its faults. Lee Edwards, the distinguished fellow in conservative thought at the Heritage Foundation, said in a presentation there, "Conservatives promise no earthly paradise but a land of ordered liberty in which the individual can go as far and as high as his ability and ambition will take him...where freedom, opportunity, prosperity, and civil society flourish."[9] When we talk about an American restoration, this is our vision.

But even though we do not aspire to make paradise on earth, we cannot ignore the necessity of a cultural belief in an underlying order to the nature of things—an order caused by divine transcendence. As Kirk asserted, a culture of individual liberty and responsibility can only occur through faith in something greater than ourselves. If we lose faith, we will lose any hope of an ordered culture. As Kirk put it, "A civilization cannot long survive the extinction of a belief in a transcendent order that brought the culture into being."[10] No restoration can occur without faith, dedication, and perseverance.

This statement of Kirk's underscores the major difference between progressives and conservatives: while conservatives look to traditional ideas—like this natural order from God—to restore society, progressives look to government. Finally, for the conservative, our Creator bestows our rights. For the progressive, the state grants rights and can take them away.

Despite the great damage already done to America's spiritual foundation, Russell Kirk remained optimistic about the future. That foundation and America's strong tradition of believing in transcendent order has given our nation a unique historical track record, one Kirk believed gave conservatives a ready-made response to progressivism. Conservatives have, in support of their convictions, "The best written constitution in the world, the safest divisions of powers, the widest diffusion of property, the strongest sense of common interest, the most prosperous economy, an elevated intellectual and moral tradition, and a spirit of self-reliance unequalled in modern times." [11]

When you add to that foundation, the "little platoons"—people who have a true understanding of what it means to be free, as defined by Pope John Paul II as "[using] one's freedom for what is a true good...to be a person of upright conscience, to be responsible, to be a person for others" [12]—you can see there is still hope we, as individuals, can positively impact our culture for good, rather than withdraw from it while cursing the darkness.

Writing in the *New York Times*, David Brooks calls these "little platoons" the "Modern Whig Party." The Whigs, which date back to the early nineteenth century, believed in promoting infrastructure projects, public education, public-private investment, and character-building projects making it possible for boys and girls from lower economic levels to succeed. He writes, "If progressives generally believe in expanding government to enhance equality, and libertarians try to reduce government to expand freedom, Whigs seek to use limited but energetic government to enhance social mobility." [13]

Brooks shares about James and Deborah Fallows, who traveled across America visiting dozens of small towns starting in Eastport, Maine, and going all the way to Redlands, California. The Fallowses found a similar story in each of these small towns: a booming industry drew workers and families to the area, then the industry collapsed, and after a period of economic difficulty, these towns are successfully rebuilding themselves into vibrant communities. They are truly in the

process of restoration that came about through citizens who are working to rebuild entrepreneurial civic institutions and churches. The
revivals are happening because these people are embracing and practicing what it means to be a civil society.

For instance, in Allentown, Pennsylvania, the Fallowses witnessed
how the community rallied around a couple who needed a foam pit
for their new gymnastics center. A local Mack Trucks factory donated
and delivered leftover padding and two hundred volunteers equipped
with electric kitchen knives rallied to carve it up into pieces. In Bend,
Oregon, the Fallowses saw AARP volunteers at the local library assist-
ing people with their taxes, while Goodwill workers taught job-seekers
resume writing. These are the "little platoons" in action and, as Brooks
points out, the towns and cities thrive because of their citizens' commitment on the local level.

Political leaders in these towns, the Fallowses noticed, are not
aspiring to run for higher office, but instead are focused on serving
their community.

Brooks writes:

> Today, in this era of local renaissance and national apoca-
> lypse, I hear people wondering if maybe America can be
> like Italy—dysfunctional on the national level but with
> strong localities and a lovely lifestyle. I don't think so.
> Local improvement can go only so far when national pol-
> itics is a meat grinder. The good news is the solutions to
> our civic problems already exist . . . we just need to take
> these civic programs and this governing philosophy and
> nationalize them. We need to transform these local stories
> into a coherent national story and a bottom-up coalition,
> which will look a lot like a 21st century descendent of the
> 19th century Whigs.[14]

In another column, Brooks shares the story of Sarah Hemminger. In high school, Sarah watched a classmate named Ryan fail his freshman year because of his deteriorating home life. She also saw six teachers rally around the young man, in some ways becoming extended family. Through their efforts, Ryan recovered, entered the U.S. Naval Academy, and became a successful young leader. He and Sarah eventually married.

Sarah went on to work on a Ph.D. in biomedical engineering at Johns Hopkins. She noticed, while being lonely in a new city, that many children in the Baltimore public schools were lonely and isolated, as well. She asked the principal at a local high school to give her the names of the kids who were struggling the most academically. She persuaded dozens of her fellow students at Johns Hopkins to join her in supporting these young men and women. Her fellow students invested in the high schoolers not just academically, but personally, by driving the kids to school, bringing them lunch, and helping with homework.

Since then, Sarah has formed an organization called Thread, which works to transform the lives of the young men and women who often fall through society's cracks. Her organization currently consists of one thousand volunteers.

She says that at first, students often reject the relationships. As one of them said, "You expect people not to be there for you." But Sarah and her volunteers persisted, and through their perseverance, they were eventually able to build trust. Sarah says, "Unconditional love is so rare in life that it is identity-changing when somebody keeps showing up even when you reject them. It is also identity-changing to be the one rejected."

That statement cuts to the essence of what it will take to restore America. It will not be done by government, either by looking to government for salvation or by totally withdrawing from government. It will not be done by withdrawing from the culture and letting its teetering foundations collapse. Restoration, both personal and corporate, will come through personal engagement with individuals and the culture that will build trust and respect over time and transform hearts and minds. In the words of Brooks, "There is no way to repair national distrust without repairing individual relationships one by one. This is where American renewal begins." [15]

In both stories, Brooks describes how individuals working in their community can facilitate a return to the "permanent things." The stories he shares are about people who have decided to engage with society rather than withdraw from it.

Thus, as people of faith, we cannot live in an either-or world. Yes, Christ's kingdom is not of this world,[16] but we are also called to be salt and light to the world[17] and to go into it to proclaim the Gospel.[18] We must continue to engage with the world while not being conformed to it.[19] We cannot simply decide that the world conforms to our faith or that we will withdraw from it and allow it to continue to collapse.

Those who profess to be Christians must take that commitment seriously in all aspects of our lives. As families, we should be studying the Scriptures and praying together. It means attending church to worship and to deepen our relationship with Christ, rather than just to be entertained. We should be teaching virtue in our homes and in our schools. We must teach that sex should be reserved for one man and one woman in a marital relationship and that male-female relationships should follow the design laid out in Ephesians 4.

How can we be instruments to restore America if we are not actively involved in the institutions that influence so much of our culture—whether government, the law, the media, the schools, or entertainment? Yes, given our current cultural and political climate, it will not be easy. But by starting in our local communities, by being intentional in our relationships with those who may not share our faith or values while never compromising them, and by engaging in our civic discourse, as Brooks notes, we can ultimately be the men and women who bring restoration to the national level, as well.

And while we may be frustrated by the current state of affairs in our society, we must be careful in our critique. Gertrude Himmelfarb warned that those who desire to purge overreaching government, in their zeal could end up belittling and delegitimizing the state. That is a dangerous proposition and goes against what it means to be a citizen called to be a participating member of the state, and not just a dissenting critic.[20]

As Himmelfarb puts it, "Today, more than ever, when there are so many legitimate grievances against government, we cannot afford to delegitimize proper government. Nor can we afford the luxury of being apolitical, of depriving ourselves of the proper resources of government."[21] Civil society, she says, requires those proper resources in order to "preserve its independence, strengthen its constituent parts, and thus re-moralize itself."[22]

Writing in the *Public Discourse,* Villanova University professor Daniel Mark outlines the problem with the argument that we should totally withdraw from government. He writes, "For those who see the ills of our society and accept that some reaction is necessary, which includes me, the debate over what to do really matters and is quite revealing. The question for Benedict-option advocates of all stripes is: What exactly do you intend in your retreat?"[23]

Mark, an Orthodox Jew, writes that this quandary is the same faced by Modern Orthodox Jews versus Ultraorthodox Jews. He states that Modern Orthodox Jews tend to gather in small neighborhoods, send their children to Jewish schools, and emphasize regular prayer. Although Ultraorthodox Jews do all that, they go even further by rejecting, in principle, all of Western culture and its values.[24]

Thus, we have the classic dilemma: one side believes government and related American institutions have become so corrupt that they are beyond redeeming, and the other side believes only government can redeem us.

On the latter view, progressives believe the government is God and they place an over-emphasis on government being the solution to our nation's problems. At the 2012 Democratic National Convention, a video was played stating, "Government is the only thing we all belong to."[25]

That is wrong, just as totally withdrawing from government is wrong. We are called to participate in government, but we all belong to God, who ordained government to benefit man.[26] When we see government as a God-ordained institution rather than a man-ordained institution, and when we see government as an instrument used by God that we, as His followers, participate in to order the affairs of man, we have the proper perspective.

Government cannot solve problems of the heart. As Mary Eberstadt writes, "millions are looking to government and their political-cultural tribes to replace what they have lost—connections to families and transcendent communities,"[27] and doing so fruitlessly. The issue is, instead, with our hearts. She adds, "Politics did not create these problems. The sexual revolution did. That's why politics will not solve them, either."[28]

She continues, "The case for hope lies elsewhere, and it begins, paradoxically, in the very debasement in which we find ourselves. There is something unnatural and inhuman about the way many human beings now pass their days. The same has also been true during other eras in history—often when society was on the verge of great renewal and reform movements.[29] Eberstadt states that the gin alleys of London led to the Victorian moral renewal. The "rough mayhem" of early America led to the Great Awakening.[30] She quotes James Q. Wilson's remarks to the American Enterprise Institute: "America has been told it would be destroyed by slavery, alcohol, subversion, immigration, civil war, economic collapse, and atom bombs, but it has survived them all." [31]

Americans are a resilient people and we have faced countless challenges as a people and have overcome them. There is no reason to believe we cannot overcome the challenges we face today.

At the beginning of the book, we quoted Edmund Burke's words about "little platoons":

> To be attached to the subdivision, to love the little platoon we belong to in society, is the first principle (the germ as it were) of public affections. It is the first link in the series by which we proceed toward a love to our country, and to mankind....We begin our public affections in our families....We pass on to our neighborhoods and our habitual provincial connections....Perhaps it is a sort of elemental training to those higher and more large regards, but which alone men can be affected, as with their own concern, in the prosperity of a kingdom.... [32]

The road to a restored America, as Burke reminds us, is not a one-way street. As Himmelfarb wrote, it takes us back to our roots to our nearest and dearest, as she called it.[33] That means looking back to the legacy bequeathed to us by our Founding Fathers. But one cannot successfully navigate a road while going in reverse. As a nation, we must continue to move forward toward a horizon illuminated by the faith that enables us to love our neighbor, invest in our communities, and appreciate the blessings of living in the freest country in the history of the world. That faith is what will bring about the renewal and regeneration we so desperately need.

John Stonestreet of the Colson Center writes:

None of this is possible, of course, without confidence in the truth of Christianity, about a confidence Abraham Kuyper was correct when he said every square inch of creation was under Christ's sovereign rule. Ultimately, the restoration of all things is God's work, not ours. We cooperate, but it is still His work. So, we have no need to worry, or fret, or to be angry when things don't go as we would like.

As Stonestreet says, we must not despair. Instead, we must continue to be faithful. The key to America's restoration is found in remaining engaged in our neighborhoods, in our communities, and in our nation—doing so faithfully and knowing God is in control. But we must be willing vessels for His service, instead of just retreating and cursing the darkness. We must look toward the examples of selfless sacrifice and emulate them in our own lives, rather than fence ourselves off from the world. If America returns to the permanent things mentioned earlier in this chapter, and if these permanent things are healthy and fortified, a healthy and fortified country will surely follow.

The challenge will still be great, but if we are bold and successful, a new American renaissance may await us.

Notes

Prologue

1. Russell Kirk, *The Conservative Mind from Burke to Eliot* (Chicago: Henry Regnery Company, 1953), 472.

2. Roger Scruton, *How to Be a Conservative* (London: Bloomsbury, 2014), 1.

3. T. S. Eliot, "Excerpts from 'Francis Herbert Bradley,'" *Times Literary Supplement*, December 29, 1927, http://tseliot.com/prose/francis-herbert-bradley.

4. T. S. Eliot, "Thoughts After Lambeth" (London: Faber & Faber, 1931).

5. Edmund Burke, *Reflections on the French Revolution*, excerpted in Charles W. Elliot, *The Harvard Classics, Vol. XXIV, Part 3* (New York: P.F. Collier & Son, 1909-14), Paragraph 75, http://www.bartleby.com/24/3/4.html.

6. G. K. Chesterton, *The Everlasting Man*, (London: Houghton & Stodden, 1925), Part II, Chapter Six.

7. Reinhold Niebuhr, *Does Society Need Religion?* (Eugene, OR: Wipf & Stock, 2010), 235-237.

8. Rod Dreher, *The Benedict Option: A Strategy for Christians in a Post-Christian Nation* (New York: Sentinel, 2017). For a good overview of the Benedict Option, we suggest: "Interview by Dr. Albert Mohler with Rod Dreher," February 13, 2017, https://albertmohler.com/2017/02/13/benedict-option-conversation-rod-dreher/.

9. James Kurth, "The American Way of Victory," *National Interest*, Summer 2000.

10. Alexis de Tocqueville, *Democracy in America*, trans. Harvey C. Mansfield and Delba Winthrop (Chicago: University of Chicago Press, 2002), 280.

11. David Brooks, "Upswingers and Downswingers," *New York Times*, October 16, 2017, p. 23, https://www.nytimes.com/2017/10/16/opinion/american-economy-progress-mobility-.html?action=click&pgtype=Homepage&clickSource=story-heading&module=opinion-c-col-left-region&region=opinion-c-col-left-region&WT.nav=opinion-c-col-left-region.

12. Stephen Prothero, "Millennials Do Faith and Politics Their Way," *USA Today*, March 29, 2010.

13. Prime Minister Winston Churchill, speech, House of Commons, June 18, 1940. Winston Churchill: His Complete Speeches, 1897-1963, ed. Robert Rhodes James, vol. 6, p. 6238.

14. T. S. Eliot, *Christianity and Culture: The Idea of a Christian Society*, (New York: Houghton-Mifflin, 1949) 27.

15. Jim "Mattress Mack" McIngvale

16. Chris and Sarah Padbury. Sarah was Craig's assistant back in the mid-1990s when he was at Focus on the Family.

17. Jessica Skropanic, "'Ocean of Compassion': Support Pours in for Couple Who Accidently Started Carr Fire," *USA Today*, August 15, 2018, https://www.usatoday.com/story/news/nation-now/2018/08/15/carr-fire-messages-support-couple-who-accidentally-started-blaze/1004016002/.

Chapter 1: Restoring America's Founding Principles

1. John Baille, *What is Christian Civilization?* (London: Oxford University Press, 1945), 59.

2. Russell Kirk, "Civilization Without Religion?" *Modern Age: A Quarterly Review*, Summer 1990.

3. Fisher Ames, Statement Concerning Education, cited in Peter Marshall and David Manual, *The Glory of America* (Bloomington, MN: Garborg's Heart 'N Home, Inc, 1991), 12.27.

4. Dennis Prager, "My Quest to Help Americans Rediscover the Bible," *Daily Signal*, January 9, 2018, https://www.dailysignal.com/2018/01/09/quest-help-americans-rediscover-bible/.

5. Ibid.

6. Ibid.

7. Cited in David Gelernter, "The Bible and American History," *Washington Times*, December 11, 2014, https://www.washingtontimes.com/news/2014/dec/11/the-bibles-influence-the-bible-and-america-history/.

8. Gabriel Sivan, *The Bible and Civilization*, (New York: Quadrangle/The New York Times Book Club Co., 2002), 236.

9. Tocqueville, *Democracy in America*, 279–280, 519.

10. Ibid., 282.

11. Ibid., 303.

12. Mark David Hall, "Faith of our Founders: The Role of Religion in America's Founding," *Intercollegiate Review Online*, Spring 2018 and Mark David Hall, "Did America Have a Christian Founding," the Heritage Foundation, June 7, 2011, http://www.heritage.org/political-process/report/did-america-have-christian-founding.

13. Abraham Lincoln, "Reply to the Colored People of Baltimore Upon Presentation of a Bible," September 7, 1864, https://albertmohler.com/2017/02/13/benedict-option-conversation-rod-dreher/.

14. Dwight D. Eisenhower, First Inaugural Address, January 20, 1953, https://www.presidency.ucsb.edu/documents/inaugural-address-3.

15. J. Fitzpatrick, ed, *The Writings of George Washington* (Washington, D.C.: U.S. Government Printing Office, 1931-39), 229.

16. Hall, "Did America Have a Christian Founding."

17. Rabbi Lord Jonathan Sacks, "Cultural Climate Change," lecture delivered at the Chautauqua Institution, July 13, 2017.

Chapter 2: Restoring Religious Liberty

1. *Baer v. Kolmorgen*, 14 Misc.2d 1015 (1958) Supreme Court, Westchester County, December 15, 1958. 14 Misc.2d 1015 (N.Y. Sup. Ct. 1958) https://www.ravellaw.com/opinions/bde4c8fbd72c7c302333631d4b8f704f.

2. "Declaration on Religious Freedom," *Dignitatis Humanae*, On the Right of the Person and of Communities to Social and Civil Freedom in Matters Religious Promulgated by His Holiness Pope Paul VI on December 7, 1964, http://www.vatican.va/archive/hist_councils/ii_vatican_council/documents/vat-ii_decl_19651207_dignitatis-humanae_en.html.

3. Archbishop Charles Chaput, "Things to Come: Faith, State, and Society in a New World," Lecture Delivered at the Matthew J. Ryan Center at Villanova University, http://www.catholicworldreport.com/2018/02/22/things-to-come-faith-state-and-society-in-a-new-world/.

4. G. K. Chesterton, *Autobiography of G. K. Chesterton*, (San Francisco: Ignatius Press, 2006), 230.

5. *Everson v. Board of Education of Ewing Township*, 330 U.S. 1 (1947).

6. *Baer v. Kolmorgen*.

7. *Wallace v. Jaffree*, 472 U.S. 38, 61 (1985).

8. Thomas Jefferson, letter to Danbury Baptists, January 1, 1802.

9. Daniel Dreisbach, *Thomas Jefferson and the Wall of Separation*, (New York: New York University Press, 2002), 29.

10. See https://www.chusa.org/about/about/facts-statistics.

11. Alexandra DeSanctis, "FiveThirtyEight Smears Catholic Hospitals," *National Review*, July 27, 2018, https://www.nationalreview.com/2018/07/catholic-hospitals-fivethirtyeight-smears-hit-piece/.

12. David French, "Why Christians Can't Compromise on Conscience," *National Review*, August 1, 2018, https://www.nationalreview.com/2018/08/catholic-hospitals-abortion-comprimise-conscience/.

13. Ibid.

14. Michael Barone, "Liberals Against Freedom of Conscience," *Washington Examiner*, August 2, 2018, https://www.washingtonexaminer.com/opinion/columnists/michael-barone-liberal-against-freedom-of-conscience.

15. Nadine Strossen, Testimony in favor of the Religious Freedom Restoration Act, September 18, 1992, 171, https://www.justice.gov/sites/default/files/jmd/legacy/2014/02/13/hear-j-102-82-1992.pdf.

16. Ibid.

17. David French, "This is How Religious Liberty Really Dies," *National Review*, February 13, 2018, https://www.nationalreview.com/2018/02/religious-liberty-threatened-culture-government/.

18. French, "Why Christians Can't Compromise Conscience."

19. Ibid.

20. Daniel Mark, "Domestic Challenges to Religious Liberty – From the Left and Right," *Public Discourse*, April 2, 2018, http://www.thepublicdiscourse.com/2018/04/21175/.

Chapter 3: Restoring Medicine and Medical Ethics

1. Philip Hawley Jr, "A Tragic Case of Modern Bioethics: Denying Life-Sustaining Treatment to a Patient Who Wanted to Live," *Public Discourse*, January 7, 2016, http://www.thepublicdiscourse.com/2016/01/16211/.

2. "The Hippocratic Oath Today," https://www.pbs.org/wgbh/nova/article/hippocratic-oath-today/.

3. Wesley J, Smith, "Forcing Doctors to Perform Abortions," *National Review*, August 8, 2018 https://www.nationalreview.com/corner/forcing-doctors-perform-abortion/.

4. Ibid.

5. International Women's Health Coalition, "Unconscionable: When Providers Deny Abortion Care," https://iwhc.org/resources/unconscionable-when-providers-deny-abortion-care/.

6. Wesley J, Smith, "Forcing Doctors to Perform Abortions."

7. "Bioethics Founder, Georgetown Professor Pellegrino Passes Away," June 18, 2013, https://www.georgetown.edu/news/pioneering-bioethicist-edmund-pellegrino-dies.html.

8. Lincoln Caplan, "Edmund Pellegrino," *Washington Post*, April 27, 1986, https://www.washingtonpost.com/archive/lifestyle/magazine/1986/04/27/edmund-pellegrino/334406d8-cf5a-4349-8655-0cdbf656f6f3/?utm_term=.0c52be5311c8.

9. For detailed info on the evil done by Dr. Mengele, see "In the Matter of Dr. Joseph Mengele: A Report to the Attorney General of the United States," U.S. Department of Justice, Criminal Division, October 1992, https://www.justice.gov/sites/default/files/criminal-hrsp/legacy/2011/02/04/10-01-92mengele-rpt.pdf.

10. Caplan, "Edmund Pellegrino."

11. Emily Langer, "Edmund Pellegrino: Bioethics Pioneer Dies at 92," *Boston Globe,* June 20, 2013, https://www.boston.com/news/education/2013/06/20/edmund-pellegrino-bioethics-pioneer-dies-at-92.

12. For Dr. Pellegrino's views on euthanasia and physician assisted suicide see Dr. Edmund Pellegrino, "Physician-Assisted Suicide and Euthanasia: Rebuttals of Rebuttals–The Moral Prohibition Remains," *Journal of Medicine and Philosophy,* 2001, https://academic.oup.com/jmp/article-abstract/26/1/93/888984?redirectedFrom=fulltext (Need subscription to access).

13. Emily Langer, "Edmund Pellegrino: Bioethics Pioneer Dies at 92."

14. Phillip Hawley Jr., "The American Medical Association vs. Human Nature," *Public Discourse,* September 6, 2017, http://www.thepublicdiscourse.com/2017/09/19980/.

15. Philip Hawley Jr., "A Tragic Case of Modern Bioethics: Denying Life-Sustaining Treatment to a Patient Who Wanted to Live."

16. Gerald T. Mundy, "Physicians Cannot Serve Both Life and Death," *Public Discourse*, January 2, 2018, http://www.thepublicdiscourse.com/2018/01/20366/.

17. Caplan, "Edmund Pellegrino."

Chapter 4: Restoring a Culture of Life

1. John Paul II, *Evangelium Vitae*, 1995, http://w2.vatican.va/content/john-paul-ii/en/encyclicals/documents/hf_jp-ii_enc_25031995_evangelium-vitae.html.

2. Number of Abortions (website), http://www.numberofabortions.com/.

3. Brittany Raymer, "A World With No Down Syndrome Babies" Focus on the Family, 2018, https://www.focusonthefamily.com/socialissues/life-issues/down-syndrome/a-world-with-no-down-syndrome-babies.

4. Wesley Smith, "Peter Singer Says an Intellectually Disabled Person is Less Valuable than Animals," *Lifenews.com*, February 27, 2017, http://www.lifenews.com/2017/02/27/peter-singer-says-an-intellectually-disabled-person-is-less-than-valuable-than-animals.

5. Ruth Marcus, "I Would Have Aborted a Fetus with Down Syndrome. Women Need That Right," *Washington Post,* March 9, 2018, https://www.washingtonpost.com/opinions/i-wouldve-aborted-a-fetus-with-down-syndrome-women-need-that-right/2018/03/09/3aaac364-23d6-11e8-94da-ebf9d112159c_story.html?utm_term=.cde0d1d65b78.

6. Ibid.

7. Sara Miller Llana, "Slippery Slope? Belgium Moves to Extend Euthanasia Rights to Children," *Christian Science Monitor,* February 13, 2014, https://www.csmonitor.com/World/Europe/2014/0213/Slippery-slope-Belgium-moves-to-extend-euthanasia-rights-to-children, and Douglas Murray, "Grim Reaper, M.D." *National Review*, April 25, 2016, https://www.nationalreview.com/2016/04/euthanasia-belgium-netherlands-slippery-slope/.

8. "A Rat Is a Pig Is a Dog Is a Boy," People for the Ethical Treatment of Animals, https://www.peta.org/blog/rat-pig-dog-boy.

9.   Elliot Hosman J.D, "The Short Life and Eugenic Death of Baby John Bollinger," *Psychology Today,* October 12, 2015, https://www.psychologytoday.com/us/blog/genetic-crossroads/201510/the-short-life-and-eugenic-death-baby-john-bollinger.

10. Kathryn Jean Lopez, "Mercy!" *National Review,* March 30, 2005.

11. Margaret Sanger, *Margaret Sanger: An Autobiography,* Chapter 30, (New York: W.W. Norton & Co., 1938) 374-375, https://archive.org/stream/margaretsangerau1938sang/margaretsangerau1938sang_djvu.txt.

12. "Apostle of Birth Control Sees Cause Gaining Here", *New York Times,* April 8, 1923, p. XII, https://www.nytimes.com/1923/04/08/archives/apostle-of-birth-control-sees-cause-gaining-here-hearing-in-albany.html.

13. Mike Wallace, Interview with Margaret Sanger, September 21, 1957, https://www.c-span.org/video/?288555-1/mike-wallace-interview-margaret-sanger.

14. Ibid.

15. "NFL Football Star Ben Watson Helps Pregnancy Center Save Babies From Abortion," *LifeNews.com,* August 7, 2018, https://www.lifenews.com/2018/08/07/nfl-football-star-ben-watson-helps-pregnancy-center-save-babies-from-abortion/.

16. Daniel Darling, "On the Brink of a Post-Roe World, Pro-Life Movement Needs a Future Beyond Abortion," *USA Today,* August 7, 2018, https://www.usatoday.com/story/opinion/2018/08/07/abortion-roe-v-wade-pro-life-movement-brett-kavanaugh-column/865843002/.

17. Ibid.

Chapter 5: Restoring Marriage, Family, and Social Capital

1.   Ronald Reagan, "Radio Address to the Nation on Family Values," December 20, 1986, http://www.presidency.ucsb.edu/ws/index.php?pid=36826.

2.   Scott Yenor, "The True Origin of Society: The Founders on the Family," the Heritage Foundation, October 16, 2013, http;//www.heritage.org/node/11602/print-display.

3. James Q. Wilson, *The Marriage Problem: How Our Culture Has Weakened Families,* (New York: Harper, 2002), 168-74.

4. Mary Eberstadt, "Two Nations, Revisited," *National Affairs,* Summer 2018, https://www.nationalaffairs.com/publications/detail/two-nations-revisited.

5. Jim Daly, "Marriage Done Right," (Washington, D.C.: Regnery Faith, 2016), xvii.

6. Wilson, *The Marriage Problem.*

7. "Births to Unmarried Women," ChildTrends Data Bank, October 2016, https://www.childtrends.org/wp-content/uploads/2015/12/75_Births_to_Unmarried_Women.pdf.

8. Ibid.

9. Ibid.

10. Ibid.

11. Robert Samuelson, "Trump is Not Destiny, Here's What Is," *Washington Post,* June 11, 2017, https://www.washingtonpost.com/opinions/trump-is-not-destiny-heres-what-is/2017/06/11/1dc9f7c6-4d33-11e7-9669-250d0b15f83b_story.html?noredirect=on&utm_term=.2d021baa9afb.

12. Yenor, "The True Origin of Society: The Founders on the Family."

13. Jason Riley, "Modern Liberalism's False Obsession with Civil War Monuments," *Wall Street Journal,* April 29, 2017, https://www.wsj.com/articles/modern-liberalisms-false-obsession-with-civil-war-monuments-1504045658.

14. Edwin J. Feulner Jr., "Assessing the Great Society," the Heritage Foundation, June 30, 2014, https://www.heritage.org/poverty-and-inequality/commentary/assessing-the-great-society.

15. "Children in Poverty," ChildTrends Data Bank, December 2016, https://www.childtrends.org/wp-content/uploads/2016/12/04_Poverty.pdf.

16. Jason Riley, "Still Right on the Black Family After All These Years," *Wall Street Journal,* February 10, 2015, https://www.wsj.com/articles/jason-l-riley-still-right-on-the-black-family-after-all-these-years-1423613625.

17. James Q, Wilson, "Why We Don't Marry," *City Journal,* Winter 2002, https://www.city-journal.org/html/why-we-don%E2%80%99t-marry-12215.html.

18.   Ibid.

19.   Ibid.

20.   Ibid.

21.   Eberstadt, "Two Nations-Revisited."

22.   Ibid.

23.   Barnini Chakraborty, "Rahm Emanuel Under Increasing Fire for Linking Chicago Violence and Morals in Minority Neighborhoods," Fox News, August 17, 2018, http://www.foxnews.com/us/2018/08/17/rahm-emanuel-under-increasing-fire-for-linking-chicago-violence-and-morals-in-minority-neighborhoods.html.

24.   Cynthia Harper and Sara S. McLanahan, "Father Absence and Youth Incarceration." *Journal of Research on Adolescence 14*, (September 2004), 369-397.

25.   "Births to Unmarried Women."

26.   "Births: Final Data for 2010," Centers for Disease Control, August 28, 2012, http://citeseerx.ist.psu.edu/viewdoc/download?doi=10.1.1.259.443&rep=rep1&type=pdf.

27.   Glenn Stanton, "The Research Proves the No. 1 Social Justice Imperative is Marriage," *Federalist*, November 3, 2017, http://thefederalist.com/2017/11/03/research-proves-no-1-social-justice-imperative-marriage/.

28.   Robert Rector, "Marriage: America's Greatest Weapon Against Child Poverty," the Heritage Foundation, September 16, 2010, https://www.heritage.org/poverty-and-inequality/report/marriage-americas-greatest-weapon-against-child-poverty-0.

29.   Peter Shuck, *One Nation Undecided: Clear Thinking about Five Hard Issues That Divide Us*, (Princeton, N.J: Princeton University Press, 2017) 44.

30.   McKenna Myers, "Fatherless Daughters: 5 Ways Growing Up Without a Dad Affects Women," July 6, 2018, https://wehavekids.com/family-relationships/When-Daddy-Dont-Love-Their-Daughters-What-Happens-to-Women-Whose-Fathers-Werent-There-for-Them.

31. Suzanne Venker, "Missing Fathers and America's Broken Boys – The Vast Majority of Mass Shooters Come from Broken Homes," Fox News, February 19, 2018, http://www.foxnews.com/opinion/2018/02/19/missing-fathers-and-americas-broken-boys-vast-majority-mass-shooters-come-from-broken-homes.html.

32. W. Bradford Wilcox and Wendy Wang, "The Class Divide in Marriage," American Enterprise Institute, September 2017, http://www.aei.org/wp-content/uploads/2017/09/The-Marriage-Divide.pdf.

33. Tim Henderson, "Growing Number of People Living Alone Can Present Challenges," *Stateline*, September 11, 2014, http://www.pewtrusts.org/en/research-and-analysis/blogs/stateline/2014/09/11/growing-number-of-people-living-solo-can-pose-challenges.

34. John Cacioppo, *Loneliness,* (New York: W.W. Norton and Company, 2008).

35. Catherine Saint Louis, "Rise in Infant Drug Dependence in U.S. is Felt Mostly in Rural Areas," *New York Times*, December 12, 2016, https://www.nytimes.com/2016/12/12/health/rise-in-infant-drug-dependence-in-us-is-felt-most-in-rural-areas.html.

36. Centers for Disease Control, "U.S. drug overdose deaths continue to rise; increase fueled by synthetic opioids," March 29, 2018, https://www.cdc.gov/media/releases/2018/p0329-drug-overdose-deaths.html.

37. National Institute on Drug Abuse, https://www.drugabuse.gov/related-topics/trends-statistics/overdose-death-rates.

38. Catherine Saint Louis, "Rise in Infant Drug Dependence in U.S. is Felt Mostly in Rural Areas."

39. "Report: Married Parents Raising Children Best Bet for Economic Prosperity of Family, Society," October 27, 2015, http://www.cnsnews.com/print/4077734.

40. Alex Hogan, "'Like you're living in hell': A survivor on what opioid withdrawal did to his body," May 5, 2015, https://www.statnews.com/2016/05/25/opioid-addiction-withdrawal-survival/.

41. Kelly Tatera, "What Happens When a Baby Is Born Addicted to Drugs? *Science Explorer,* December 16, 2015, http://thescienceexplorer.com/brain-and-body/what-happens-when-baby-born-addicted-drugs.

42. Hannah Rappleye, Rich McHugh, and Ronan Farrow, "Born Addicted: The Number of Opioid Addicted Babies is Soaring," NBC News, October 9, 2017, https://www.nbcnews.com/storyline/americas-heroin-epidemic/born-addicted-number-opioid-addicted-babies-soaring-n806346.

43. Nicholas Zill, "Substance Abuse, Mental Illness, and Crime More Common in Disrupted Families," Institute for Family Studies, March 24, 2015, https://ifstudies.org/blog/substance-abuse-mental-illness-and-crime-more-common-in-disrupted-families.

44. Timothy P. Carney, "Failing Families," *Washington Examiner,* June 26, 2018, https://www.washingtonexaminer.com/opinion/american-culture-is-moving-into-a-post-family-era.

45. Tyler J. VanderWeele, "Religious Service Attendance, Marriage, and Health," Institute for Family Studies, November 29, 2016, https://ifstudies.org/blog/religious-service-attendance-marriage-and-health/.

46. Kenneth Pargament and Annette Mahoney, "Sacred Matters: The Spiritual Dimensions of Marital and Family Ties," Bowling Green University cited in David Yonke, "Happy Marriage Begins at Church Door, BGSU Report Finds," *Toledo Blade,* April 14, 2007, http://www.toledoblade.com/Religion/2007/04/14/Happy-marriage-begins-at-church-door-BGSU-study-reports.html.

47. VanderWeele, "Religious Service Attendance, Marriage, and Health."

48. Glenn Stanton, "Does Faith Reduce Divorce Risk?" *Public Discourse,* March 22, 2018, http://www.thepublicdiscourse.com/2018/03/20935/.

49. Wilson, "Why We Don't Marry."

50. W. Bradford Wilcox and Wendy Wang, "The Class Divide in Marriage."

51. "Five Key Findings on Religion in the U.S." Gallup.com, December 23, 2016, https://news.gallup.com/poll/200186/five-key-findings-religion.aspx.

52. Josh McDowell, *Why True Love Waits: A Definitive Book on How to Help Your Youth Resist Sexual Pressure* (Carol Stream, IL: Tyndale House Publishers 2002), 158.

53. "Foster Care & Adoption," Focus on the Family (website), https://www.focusonthefamily.com/pro-life/orphan-care.

54. Project 1.27 (website), https://www.project127.com/.

55. Bethany Christian Services (website), https://www.bethany.org/.

Chapter 6: Restoring the Concept of the Gentleman

1. Edmund Burke, *Reflections on the French Revolution*, (Boston: The Harvard Classics, 1909-1914), Paragraphs 125-149, https://www.bartleby.com/24/3/6.html.

2. Cardinal John Henry Newman, "The Idea of the University," (Notre Dame, IN: University of Notre Dame Press, 1982), 180-181.

3. George Gilder, *Men and Marriage*, (Gretna, LA: Pelican Publishing, 1986), 17.

4. Ibid.

5. Peggy Noonan, "America Needs More Gentleman," *Wall Street Journal*, January 18, 2018, https://www.wsj.com/articles/america-needs-more-gentlemen-1516320167.

6. Ibid.

7. Ibid.

8. Ben Shapiro, "Men, Stop Virtue-Signaling and Return to Rules," *National Review*, November 21, 2017, http://www.nationalreview.com/node/453962/print.

9. Ibid.

10. Ibid.

11. C. S. Lewis, *The Abolition of Man*, (London: Oxford University Press,1943), 26.

12. Fay Vincent, "'Always Be a Gentleman' and Other Fatherly Advice," *Wall Street Journal*, June 13, 2013, https://www.wsj.com/articles/SB10000872396390443675404578056291818726864.

Chapter 7: Restoring Virtue

1.   Edmund Burke, *Reflections on the French Revolution*.

2.   John Adams, "To the Inhabitants of the Massachusetts-Bay," February 6, 1775, http://www.masshist.org/publications/adams-papers/view?id=A DMS-06-02-02-0072-0004.

3.   Christine Emba, "Let's Rethink Sex," *Washington Post*, November 26, 2017, https://www.washingtonpost.com/opinions/lets-rethink-sex/2017/11/26/ d8546a86-d2d5-11e7-b62d-d9345ced896d_story.html?noredirect=on&utm_ term=.5f298e0a2bfa.

4.   Cal Thomas, "The Return of Virtue," *Washington Times*, November 29, 2017, https://www.washingtontimes.com/news/2017/nov/29/the-value-of-high-moral-standards-has-never-been-m/.

5.   Lewis, *The Abolition of Man*.

6.   Harry Stein and Kay S. Hymowitz, "Earth to Ivory Tower: Get Real!" *City Journal*, Autumn 2001, https://www.city-journal.org/html/earth-ivory-tower-get-real-12201.html .

7.   Jared Sparks, ed., *The Writings of Benjamin Franklin*, (Boston: Tappan, Whittemore and Mason, Boston, 1840), Vol. 10, 297.

8.   "Saint Thomas Aquinas on Virtues," http://www.aquinasonline.com/Topics/ virtues.html.

9.   Aristotle, *Nicomachean Ethics*, Book III, Chapter 11, 1118b-1119a.

10. Aristotle, *Politica*, 1129 a. 6 f.

11. John A. Hardon, *Modern Catholic Dictionary*, (Bardstown, KY: Eternal Life Publications, 2000).

Chapter 8: Restoring Education

1.   G. K. Chesterton, *The Common Man*, (London: Sheed & Ward, 1950), 166.

2.   William Bennett, forward in Josiah Bunting, *An Education for Our Time*, (Washington, D.C: Regnery Publishing, 1998), xv.

3.   Ulrich Boser, Perpetual Baffour, and Steph Vela, "A Look at the Education Crisis: Tests, Standards, and the Future of American Education," January 2016,

https://cdn.americanprogress.org/wp-content/uploads/2016/01/26105959/
TUDAreport2.pdf.

4. Kevin Roberts, "How to Fix American Schools," March 16, 2017, http://www.
theamericanconservative.com/articles/how-to-fix-american-schools/.

5. Kimberly Amadeo, "U.S. Education Ranking is Falling Behind the Rest of the
World," May 11, 2018, https://www.thebalance.com/the-u-s-is-losing-its-
competitive-advantage-3306225.

6. "2015 Reading Trial Urban District Snapshot Report Detroit Grade 8," https://
nces.ed.gov/nationsreportcard/subject/publications/dst2015/pdf/2016048XR8.
pdf.

7. Ibid.

8. For detailed information on this issue see: Richard Arum, "Academically
Adrift: Limited Learning on College Campuses," (Chicago: University of
Chicago Press), 2011.

9. Craig Silverman, "Here are 50 of the Biggest Fake News Hits on Facebook
From 2016," https://www.buzzfeed.com/craigsilverman/top-fake-news-of-
2016?utm_term=.jiznNzzEV#.rlaJjbbeO.

10. "Dig Deeper: Critical Thinking in the Digital Age," https://mindedge.com/
page/dig-deeper.

11. George A. Panichas, "School and Society: A Conservative Perspective,"
Intercollegiate Studies Institute, Vol. 48, No. 2, Spring 2006, https://home.isi.
org/school-and-society-conservative-perspective.

12. James Coleman, et al, "Equality of Educational Opportunity," National Center
for Educational Statistics, https://files.eric.ed.gov/fulltext/ED012275.pdf.

13. Robert Putnam, *Bowling Alone: The Collapse and Revival of American
Community* (New York: Simon and Schuster), 2000, cited in Karen
Bogenschneider and Carol Johnson, "Family Involvement in Education: How
Important Is It? What Can Legislators Do? Policy Institute for Family Impact
Seminars, February 2004, https://www.purdue.edu/hhs/hdfs/fii/wp-content/
uploads/2015/06/fia_brchapter_20c02.pdf.

14. Laurence Steinberg, *Why School Reform Has Failed and What Parents Need to Do,"* (New York: Simon and Schuster, 1996), cited in Bogenschneider and Johnson, "Family Involvement in Education."

15. Karen Bogenschneider and Carol Johnson, "Family Involvement in Education."

16. "The Math on School Meals," *New York Times*, September 5, 2017, https://www.nytimes.com/2017/09/05/dining/school-lunch-data.html.

17. For examples, see Dan Lips, "Teachers Unions Block School Choice," *Salt Lake City Tribune,* November 13, 2007, https://www.heritage.org/education/report/teachers-unions-block-school-choice, Jason Bedrick, "Obama's War on School Choice," *National Review,* January 28, 2016, https://www.nationalreview.com/2016/01/barack-obama-school-choice-war/, and "Milwaukee May Create Zoning Rule to Block School Choice," Education Action Group Foundation, July 18, 2012, http://eagnews.org/milwaukee-may-create-zoning-rule-to-block-school-choice/.

18. John Dewey, "Sense of Power Is Aim" speech given at Teachers College, Columbia University reprinted in *New York Times,* August 23, 1933, http://www.yorku.ca/rsheese2/3410/utopia.htm.

19. Chris Talgo and Lennie Jarratt, "Government Can't Cure Our Education Problem, Only Parental Choice Can," *American Thinker,* June 3, 2018, https://www.americanthinker.com/articles/2018/06/government_cant_cure_our_education_problem_only_parental_choice_can.html.

20. Ibid.

21. George Will, "A California Election That Might Actually Matter," *Washington Post,* August 1, 2018, https://www.washingtonpost.com/opinions/a-california-election-that-might-actually-matter/2018/07/31/6a046e70-94e8-11e8-80e1-00e80e1fdf43_story.html?utm_term=.ad5632db757b.

Chapter 9: Restoring Civility

1. David French, "Civility Isn't Surrender," *National Review,* March 9, 2018, https://www.nationalreview.com/2018/03/civility-isnt-surrender/.

2. Louis Sarkozy, "No One Knows How to Agree to Disagree Anymore," *Washington Examiner,* July 25, 2018, https://www.washingtonexaminer.com/opinion/no-one-knows-how-to-agree-to-disagree-anymore.

3. Victor Davis Hanson, "The Origins of our Second Civil War," *National Review,* July 31, 2018, https://www.nationalreview.com/2018/07/origins-of-second-civil-war-globalism-tech-boom-immigration-campus-radicalism/.

4. Barack Obama, Remarks at the 100th Birthday of Nelson Mandela, July 18, 2018, https://www.independent.co.uk/news/world/americas/barack-obama-speech-in-full-nelson-mandela-lecture-transcript-south-africa-a8452331.html.

5. Arthur Brooks, "Empathize with Your Political Foe," *New York Times,* January 22, 2018, http://www.aei.org/publication/empathize-with-your-political-foe/.

6. Ibid.

7. Richard Reeves, "Trickle-Down Norms," *National Affairs,* Winter 2018, 123-134, https://www.nationalaffairs.com/publications/detail/trickle-down-norms.

8. Gary Varvel, "Why America is So Uncivil and How to Fix It," *Indianapolis Star,* June 25, 2018, https://www.indystar.com/story/opinion/columnists/varvel/2018/06/25/varvel-why-america-so-uncivil-and-how-fix/730740002/.

9. Text of John Edwards's Speech to the Democratic National Convention, July 28, 2004, http://www.washingtonpost.com/wp-dyn/articles/A22230-2004Jul28.html.

10. "The Partisan Divide on Political Values Grows Even Wider," http://www.people-press.org/2017/10/05/the-partisan-divide-on-political-values-grows-even-wider/.

11. Ibid.

12. Lara Brown, "State of American Democracy," *Hill,* May 1, 2018, http://thehill.com/opinion/campaign/385469-the-state-of-american-democracy-mean.

13. Ibid.

14. Ibid.

15. Ibid.

16. Glenn Harlan Reynolds, "Is America Headed Toward a Civil War?" *USA Today,* June 25, 2018, https://www.usatoday.com/story/opinion/2018/06/25/

sanders-nielsen-incidents-suggest-new-us-civil-war-underway-
   column/729141002/ .

17.   Jeremy W. Peters "If You Think the Political Divide is Worse Than Ever, You
      May Be Right," *Seattle Times*, August 17, 2018, https://www.seattletimes.com/
      nation-world/if-you-think-the-political-divide-is-worse-than-ever-you-may-
      be-right/.

18.   Ibid.

19.   Ibid.

20.   "31% Think U.S. Civil War Likely Soon," *Rasmussen Reports*, June 27, 2018,
      http://www.rasmussenreports.com/public_content/politics/general_politics/
      june_2018/31_think_u_s_civil_war_likely_soon.

21.   Paul Bedard, "Poll: 39 Percent Back Secession, Strongest Among Democrats,
      Blacks," *Washington Examiner*, August 12, 2018, https://www.
      washingtonexaminer.com/washington-secrets/poll-39-back-secession-
      strongest-among-democrats-blacks.

22.   Reynolds, "Is America Headed Toward a Civil War."

23.   Janet Hook, "Political Divisions in U.S. are Widening, Long-Lasting, Poll
      Shows," *Wall Street Journal*, September 6, 2017, https://www.wsj.com/articles/
      political-divisions-in-u-s-are-widening-long-lasting-poll-shows-1504670461.

24.   Ibid.

25.   Hanson, "The Origins of our Second Civil War."

26.   "Read Hillary Clinton's 'Basket of Deplorables' Remarks About Donald Trump
      Supporters," *Time*, September 10, 2016, http://time.com/4486502/hillary-
      clinton-basket-of-deplorables-transcript/.

27.   Sarkozy, "No One Knows How to Agree to Disagree Anymore."

28.   See Number 1593, Benjamin Franklin, http://www.bartleby.com/73/1593.html.

29.   "The Caning of Senator Charles Sumner," https://www.senate.gov/
      artandhistory/history/minute/The_Caning_of_Senator_Charles_Sumner.
      htm.

30. Kate Nocera and Lissandra Villa, "The 9 Minutes that Almost Changed America," *BuzzFeed*, May 14, 2018, https://www.buzzfeed.com/katenocera/baseball-shooting?utm_term=.sy5EWmvxwM#.nrRbwjAOWZ.

31. Examples include Joe Berkowitz, "It's Your Civic Duty to Ruin Thanksgiving by Bringing Up Trump," *GQ*, November 21, 2017, https://www.gq.com/story/the-case-for-ruining-thanksgiving, Peter Van Buren, "How to Talk with Trump-Hating Millennials This Thanksgiving," *American Conservative*, November 22, 2017, http://www.theamericanconservative.com/articles/how-to-talk-to-trump-hating-millennials-this-thankgiving/, Derrick Lemos, "This Thanksgiving, Stand Up to Your Relatives Who Helped Elect Trump," *Establishment*, November 10, 2016, https://theestablishment.co/your-friends-and-relatives-did-this-now-what-can-you-do-695ff8ddc260.

32. Berkowitz.

33. French, "Civility isn't Surrender," *National Review*.

34. Chuck Colson, "Embracing Courtesy," *BreakPoint*, January 10, 2011, http://www.breakpoint.org/2017/07/breakpoint-embracing-courtesy-2/.

35. Brit Hume, "Maxine Waters Needs to Keep a Civil Tongue and So Do We All."

36. Hanson, "The Origins of our Second Civil War."

37. Varvel, "Why America is So Uncivil and How to Fix It."

38. Sarkozy, "No One Knows How to Agree to Disagree Anymore."

39. Thomas O'Neill, "Frenemies: A Love Story," *New York Times*, October 5, 2012, http://campaignstops.blogs.nytimes.com/2012/10/05/frenemies-a-love-story/.

40. Neal Urwitz and Harry J. Kazianis, "Political Hatred Has Gone Wild – Americans Need to Work Together," Fox News, August 8, 2018, http://www.foxnews.com/opinion/2018/08/08/political-hatred-has-gone-wild-americans-need-to-work-together.html.

41. Brooks, "Empathize with Your Political Foe."

Chapter 10: Restoring Citizenship and Duty

1. Russell Kirk, "The Marriage of Rights and Duties," *Intercollegiate Review,* Spring 1992, http://www.theimaginativeconservative.org/2012/02/russell-kirk-marriage-of-rights-and-duties.html.

2. Dwight D. Eisenhower, First Inaugural Address, January 20, 1953, https://www.eisenhower.archives.gov/research/online_documents/inauguration_1953/1953_01_20_Inaugural_Address.pdf.

3. Daniel Webster, "Speech on the 200th Anniversary of the Landing at Plymouth Rock," December 22, 1820, https://www.dartmouth.edu/~dwebster/speeches/plymouth-oration.html.

4. Russell Kirk, ed. "Orestes Brownson: Selected Political Essays," (New Brunswick, N.J.:Transaction Publishers, 1990), 2.

5. Tom Ziglar, "Gratitude Creates Integrity," https://www.ziglar.com/articles/gratitude-creates-integrity/.

6. US Debt Clock (website), http://www.usdebtclock.org/.

7. Aleksandr Solzhenitsyn, *The Gulag Archipelago* 1918-1956, (1973).

8. Jennifer Breheny Wallace, "How to Raise More Grateful Children," *Wall Street Journal*, February 23, 2018.

9. Poll cited in ibid.

10. Ibid.

11. Ibid.

12. Ibid.

13. Brit Hume, "Zogby Poll: Most Americans Can Name Three Stooges But Not Three Branches of Government," Fox News, August 15, 2006, http://www.foxnews.com/story/2006/08/15/zogby-poll-most-americans-can-name-three-stooges-but-not-three-branches-govt.html.

14. "State of the First Amendment," https://www.freedomforuminstitute.org/first-amendment-center/state-of-the-first-amendment/.

15. Stephen Macedo, "Crafting Good Citizens," *Education Next,* Sprint 2004, http://educationnext.org/files/ednext20042_10.pdf.

16. Adam Taylor, "American Voter Turnout is Still Lower than Most Other Wealthy Nations," *Washington Post*, November 10, 2016, https://www. washingtonpost.com/news/worldviews/wp/2016/11/10/even-in-a-historic-election-americans-dont-vote-as-much-as-those-from-other-nations/?noredirect=on&utm_term=.5eb7663050c3.

17. "Three Methods Of Reform" in *Pamphlets: Translated from the Russian* (1900) as translated by Aylmer Maude, 29.

18. Justice Clarence Thomas, "Freedom and Obligation," Commencement Address at Hillsdale College, May 14, 2016, https://imprimis.hillsdale.edu/freedom-obligation-2016-commencement-address/.

19. Abraham Lincoln, State of the Union address, December 3, 1861, http://presidentialrhetoric.com/historicspeeches/lincoln/stateoftheunion1861.html.

20. Wallace, "How to Raise More Grateful Children."

21. Ronald Reagan, "Farewell Address to the Nation," January 11, 1989, https://www.reaganlibrary.gov/01189i.

22. Ibid.

Chapter 11: Restoring Community

1. Dan Edmunds, "Distress and the Breakdown of Community," *Psychology Today*, March 4, 2013, https://www.psychologytoday.com/us/blog/extreme-states-mind/201304/distress-and-the-breakdown-community?quicktabs_5=1.

2. *It's a Wonderful Life*, 1946, Liberty Films.

3. Tocqueville, *Democracy in America*.

4. Ben Shapiro, "On the Super Bowl and the Social Fabric," *CNSNews.com*, February 8, 2018, https://cnsnews.com/print/20641777.

5. Cheryl Stutzman, "Don't Be a Stranger," *Washington Times*, August 19, 2014, https://www.washingtontimes.com/news/2014/aug/19/stutzman-don't-be-stranger.

6. Meaghan McDonough, "We Don't Know Our Neighbors Anymore. Here's What That Costs Us," *Boston Globe Magazine*, October 10, 2017, https://www.

bostonglobe.com/magazine/2017/10/10/don-know-our-neighbors-anymore-here-what-that-costs/m9sTUVbmi3XFfxRN96Ft9M/story.html.

7.   Tyler Schmall, "Millennials Don't Know Their Neighbors at All," *New York Post*, July 10, 2018, https://nypost.com/2018/07/10/millennials-are-horrible-neighbors/.

8.   Peter Lovenheim, "How Well Do You Know Your Neighbors?" *Washington Post*, May 10, 2013, https://www.washingtonpost.com/opinions/how-well-do-you-know-your-neighbors/2013/05/10/1d1488da-b824-11e2-92f3-f291801936b8_story.html?utm_term=.59f19fcbbc9b.

9.   "Learner's Dictionary," Merriam-Webster (website), http://www.learnersdictionary.com/definition/tribalism.

10. Cited by David Brooke, "The Retreat to Tribalism," *New York Times*, January 1, 2018, https://www.nytimes.com/2018/01/01/opinion/the-retreat-to-tribalism.html.

11. Andrew Sullivan, "America Wasn't Built for Humans," *New York Magazine*, September 19, 2017, http://nymag.com/daily/intelligencer/2017/09/can-democracy-survive-tribalism.html (Retrieved July 16, 2018).

12. "The Great Decline: 60 Years of Religion in One Graph," *Religion News Service*, January 27, 2014, https://religionnews.com/2014/01/27/great-decline-religion-united-states-one-graph/.

13. Leeta-Rose Ballester, "Service Clubs Have Suffered Declining Membership in the Past 30 Years," *San Jose Mercury-News*, August 27, 2014, https://www.mercurynews.com/2014/08/27/service-clubs-have-suffered-declining-membership-in-the-past-30-years/ and Active Participation in Voluntary Organizations Declining Faster Than Checkbooks Can Keep Up," *UT News*, August 23, 2011, https://news.utexas.edu/2011/08/23/sociology_paxton_associations.

14. Salena Zito, "America's Dearth of Civil Society," *Washington Examiner*, June 26, 2018, https://www.washingtonexaminer.com/opinion/columnists/salena-zito-americas-dearth-of-civil-society.

15. Emma Green, "The Quiet Religious Freedom Fight That is Remaking America," *Atlantic*, November 2017, https://www.theatlantic.com/politics/archive/2017/11/rluipa/543504/.

16. David Davenport and Hanna Skandera, "Civic Associations," https://www.hoover.org/sites/default/files/uploads/documents/0817939628_59.pdf.

17. Inaugural address of President John F. Kennedy, Washington, D.C., January 20, 1961, https://www.jfklibrary.org/Research/Research-Aids/Ready-Reference/JFK-Quotations/Inaugural-Address.aspx.

18. Ibid.

19. Fred Bauer, "How to Renew Our Civic Culture," *National Review*, October 20, 2017, https://www.nationalreview.com/2017/10/renewing-civic-culture-politics-less-tribalism-moralism-more-community-ethics/.

Chapter 12: Restoring the Balance between Politics and Culture

1. "The Great Seduction of Modern Politics," http://www.estatevaults.com/bol/archives/2009/09/22/the_great_seduc.html.

2. Richard Weaver, *Ideas Have Consequences,* (Chicago: University of Chicago Press, 1948) 33-34.

3. See U.S. Debt Clock, http://www.usdebtclock.org/.

4. C. Northcote Parkinson, *The Law of Longer Life,* (Troy, AL: Troy State University Press, 1978).

5. Robert Bork, *Slouching Towards Gomorrah,* (New York: Regan Books, 1996).

6. Jesse Norman, "Edmund Burke – The great conservative who foresaw the discontents of our era," *Telegraph,* May 9, 2013 https://www.telegraph.co.uk/history/10046562/Edmund-Burke-the-great-conservative-who-foresaw-the-discontents-of-our-era.html.

7. John Stonestreet, "Let's Talk About Christians and Politics," *BreakPoint,* February 26, 2018 http://www.breakpoint.org/2018/02/breakpoint-lets-talk-about-christians-and-politics/.

8. David Dayen, "The 'Deplorables' Got the Last Laugh," *New Republic,* November 9, 2016 https://newrepublic.com/article/138615/deplorables-got-last-laugh.

9. "Blaine Amendments," http://ij.org/issues/school-choice/blaine-amendments/.

10. "Timothy Leary," https://www.biography.com/people/timothy-leary-37330.

11. Adam Gopnick, "Hugh Hefner, Playboy, and the American Male," *New Yorker,* September 29, 2017 https://www.newyorker.com/news/daily-comment/hugh-hefner-playboy-and-the-american-male.

12. Roger Kimball, "What the Sixties Brought," January 23, 2008 https://www.weltwoche.ch/ausgaben/2008-4/artikel/artikel-2008-04-what-the-sixties-brought.html.

13. David Masci and Michael Lipka, "Where Christian Churches, Other Religions Stand on Gay Marriage," Pew Research Center, December 21, 2015 http://www.pewresearch.org/fact-tank/2015/12/21/where-christian-churches-stand-on-gay-marriage/.

14. W. Bradford Wilcox, "The Evolution of Divorce," *National Affairs,* Fall 2009 https://www.nationalaffairs.com/publications/detail/the-evolution-of-divorce.

15. Jason Willick, "The Man Who Discovered 'Culture Wars,'" *Wall Street Journal,* May 25, 2018 https://www.wsj.com/articles/the-man-who-discovered-culture-wars-1527286035.

16. Ronald Reagan, "National Affairs Campaign Address On Religious Liberty," August 22, 1980, http://americanrhetoric.com/speeches/ronaldreaganreligiousliberty.htm.

17. Alex Roraty, "Abortion Debate is Over in the Democratic Party," *McClatchy Newspapers,* March 13, 2018 https://www.mcclatchydc.com/news/politics-government/article204751989.html.

18. "Interview by Dr. Albert Mohler with Rod Dreher," February 13, 2017, op.cit.

19. Jonah Goldberg, "Politics Can't Fill the Holes in Our Souls," *National Review,* June 27, 2018 https://www.nationalreview.com/2018/06/when-partisan-identity-like-religion-bad-for-america/.

20. Ibid.

Chapter 13: Restoring the Constitution

1. Matthew Spalding, *We Still Hold These Truths,* (Wilmington, Delaware: ISI Books, 2009), 99.

2. Charles Evans Hughes, Speech before the Chamber of Commerce, Elmira, New York, May 3, 1907, published in *Addresses and Papers of Charles Evans Hughes, Governor of New York, 1906–1908* (1908), 139.

3. James Madison, "The Particular Structure of the New Government and the Distribution of Power Among Its Different Parts," *The Federalist* No. 47, February 1, 1788, https://www.congress.gov/resources/display/content/The+Federalist+Papers#TheFederalistPapers-47.

4. Clarence Thomas, "Be Not Afraid," Speech at the American Enterprise Institute, Washington, D.C., February 13, 2001, http://www.aei.org/publication/be-not-afraid/.

5. Jack M. Balkin and Reva B. Siegel, *The Constitution in 2020,* (London: Oxford University Press, 2009).

6. Woodrow Wilson, "The New Freedom," Chapters 1 and 2, 1913, http://teachingamericanhistory.org/library/document/the-new-freedom/.

7. Ronald J. Pestritto, "Woodrow Wilson: Godfather of Liberalism," the Heritage Foundation, *First Principles,* No. 1, July 31, 2012, http://thf_media.s3.amazonaws.com/2012/pdf/PB01.pdf.

8. *Griswold v. Connecticut,* 381 U.S. 479 (1965).

9. *Planned Parenthood v. Casey* 505 U.S. 833 (1992), https://supreme.justia.com/cases/federal/us/505/833/case.pdf.

10. Speech by Attorney General Edwin Meese, III before The Federalist Society Lawyers Division on November 15, 1985, https://fedsoc.org/commentary/publications/the-great-debate-attorney-general-ed-meese-iii-november-15-1985.

11. Antonin Scalia, "Constitution Interpretation," Wilson Center, March 13, 2005, https://www.c-span.org/video/?185883-1/constitutional-interpretation.

12. "From John Adams to Massachusetts Militia, 11 October 1798," *Founders Online*, National Archives, last modified November 26, 2017, http://founders. archive.gov/documents/Adams/99-02-3102.

13. *Marbury v. Madison*, 5 U.S. (1 Cranch) 137 (1803).

14. *Roe v. Wade*, https://www.history.com/topics/roe-v-wade.

15. Scalia, "Constitution Interpretation."

16. Adam J. White, "Soulcraft as Statecraft," *Weekly Standard*, October 9, 2017, https://www.weeklystandard.com/adam-j-white/soulcraft-as-statecraft.

17. Peggy Lamson, *Roger Baldwin: Founder of the American Civil Liberties Union*, (Boston: Houghton-Mifflin, 1976), 51.

18. Victor Davis Hanson, "Ten Commandments of the Supreme Court," *National Review*, July 17, 2018, https://www.nationalreview.com/2018/07/supreme-court-whatever-advances-progressive-causes-is-sacrosanct/.

19. "Read the Statements of Supreme Court Justices on Antonin Scalia's Death," *Washington Post*, February 14, 2016, https://www.washingtonpost.com/news/post-nation/wp/2016/02/14/read-the-statements-of-supreme-court-justices-on-antonin-scalias-death/?utm_term=.59d6655a21f2.

20. Scalia, Speech to Archbishop Rummel High School, Metairie, Louisiana, January 2, 2016, https://www.nola.com/politics/index.ssf/2016/01/listen_to_justice_antonin_scal.html.

Chapter 14: Restoring Patriotism and Sacrifice

1. Bradley Lecture: Walter Berns on Patriotism, September 16, 1996, http://www. citizenship-aei.org/1996/09/bradley-lecture-walter-berns-on-patriotism/#. W4bEbuhKiUk.

2. Irving Berlin, *St. James Encyclopedia of Popular Culture: Five Volumes*, (Farmington Hills, MI: St. James Press, 2000). See http://www.pbs.org/wnet/broadway/stars/irving-berlin/.

3. Lydia Hutchinson, "Irving Berlin's 'God Bless America,'" May 11, 2014, http://performingsongwriter.com/god-bless-america/.

4. Michael E. Ruane, "Long entombed at National Cathedral, a forgotten hero of WWI is recalled," *Washington Post,* October 13, 2016, https://www. washingtonpost.com/local/long-entombed-at-national-cathedral-a-forgotten-hero-of-wwi-is-recalled/2016/10/12/c8bd2fc4-8fd6-11e6-9c85-ac42097b8cc0_ story.html?utm_term=.4c72df697149.

5. Ibid.

6. "From Peace to Patriotism: The Shifting Identity of 'God Bless America,'" Interview of Sheryl Kaskowitz by Robert Siegel, *National Public Radio,* September 2, 2013, https://www.npr.org/2013/09/02/216877219/from-peace-to-patriotism-the-shifting-identity-of-god-bless-america.

7. Peggy Noonan, "The Spirit of America is Alive in Texas," *Wall Street Journal,* August 31, 2017, https://www.wsj.com/articles/the-american-spirit-is-alive-in-texas-1504221483.

Chapter 15: Restoring America

1. Franklin Delano Roosevelt, "Radio Address Before the Eighth Pan American Scientific Congress. Washington, D.C., May 10, 1940," http://www.presidency. ucsb.edu/ws/index.php?pid=15948.

2. Ronald Reagan, "Remarks in New Orleans, Louisiana, at the Annual Meeting of the International Association of Chiefs of Police, September 28, 1981," http:// www.presidency.ucsb.edu/ws/?pid=44300.

3. Aleksandr Solzhenitsyn, "A World Split Apart," Harvard University, June 8, 1978, https://www.americanrhetoric.com/speeches/ alexandersolzhenitsynharvard.htm.

4. T. S. Eliot, *Christianity and Culture: The Idea of a Christian Society,* op.cit. 76.

5. Roger Scruton, *Liberty and Civilization: The Western Heritage,* (New York: Encounter Books, 2010), vii.

6. Ibid.

7. Russell Kirk, "Is Life Worth Living?" found in *The Sword of Imagination: Memoirs of a Half-Century of Literary Conflict,* (Grand Rapids, MI: Eerdmans, 1995), 471-76.

8. Cited by Lee Edwards in "Our Cultural Crisis: A Kirkian Response," speech delivered at the Heritage Foundation, March 14, 2018, https://www.heritage.org/conservatism/commentary/our-cultural-crisis-kirkian-response.

9. Ibid.

10. Ibid.

11. Ibid.

12. Pope John Paul II, Dilecti Amici, (To the Youth of the World), Apostolic Letter dated March 31, 1985, https://www.catholicnewsagency.com/document/dilecti-amici-to-the-youth-of-the-world-686.

13. David Brooks, "The American Renaissance Is Already Happening," *New York Times*, May 14, 2018, https://www.nytimes.com/2018/05/14/opinion/the-american-renaissance-is-already-happening.html.

14. Ibid.

15. Brooks, "Where American Renewal Begins," *New York Times*, July 26, 2018, https://www.nytimes.com/2018/07/26/opinion/thread-baltimore-american-renewal-community-program.html.

16. John 18:36.

17. Matthew 5:14.

18. Mark 16:15.

19. Romans 12:2.

20. Gertrude Himmelfarb, "For the Love of Country," *Commentary Magazine,* May 1, 1997, https://www.commentarymagazine.com/articles/for-the-love-of-country-2/.

21. Ibid.

22. Ibid.

23. Mark, "Domestic Challenges to Religious Liberty—From the Left and Right."

24. Ibid.

25. See https://www.buzzfeednews.com/article/buzzfeedpolitics/government-is-the-only-thing-we-all-belong-to.

26. Romans 13:1.

27. Eberstadt, "Two Nations—Revisited."

28. Ibid.

29. Ibid.

30. Ibid.

31. Ibid.

32. Burke, *Reflections on the French Revolution*, para. 75.

33. Himmelfarb, "For the Love of Country."

Index